Israel Thorndike,
Federalist Financier

Portrait of Israel Thorndike by Gilbert Stuart,
about 1820
(*In the possession of Dr. Augustus Thorndike, Boston*)

Israel Thorndike,
Federalist Financier

BY

J. D. FORBES

EXPOSITION — UNIVERSITY BOOK

Published *for*

THE BEVERLY HISTORICAL SOCIETY

by

EXPOSITION PRESS • NEW YORK

FIRST EDITION

475

For three generations of Abbotts

This biography is published under the imprint of the Beverly Historical Society to further the awareness of Beverly's contribution to the development of the United States.

Preface

Israel Thorndike was a businessman in Massachusetts during the period of the Revolutionary War and the Napoleonic Wars and their aftermath. His career was active and colorful enough to be worth examining on its own account. The man's peculiar significance, however, lies in the fact that he came close to being the archetype of his species in the given place and time.

The Thorndike story follows a classic pattern. From modest origins Israel chose the most rapid and at the same time the most daring course to achieve fortune. He went to sea at an early age. After his active seafaring he became a shipowner and merchant and wound up as a financier with venture capital ready to invest in a wide variety of enterprises.

His career coincided with the transition of New England from an essentially maritime community to a manufacturing area. In that transition Thorndike had a considerable part. It was the money acquired in maritime trade that he and his associates put into textiles and metals and new means of overland transportation. In this investment trend was partly re-enacted the larger, older story of the change-over of the mother country England from a commercial to an industrial state.

Thorndike's business life also coincided with the culmination and subsequent decline of the smaller seaport towns of New England as independent centers of overseas trade. He saw his native Beverly rise from a fishing village to a flourishing deep-sea port only to sink back into obscurity when Boston absorbed the commerce of the region roundabout—to lose most of it, in turn, to her better situated rival New York. Thorndike's own removal from Beverly to Boston in the year 1810, as well as his subsequent identification with the metropolis, was an expression of that economic shift.

Israel Thorndike was a key figure in the business and social and political life of Essex County and of Boston for more than half a century, as countless references of the time attest. But he was a man of action, not of contemplation. Like most men of affairs he did not set down his reasons for doing things. Undoubtedly he often acted on an intuitive estimate of the situation and so could not have stated his reasons if he had wanted to. It is at times frustrating to find the evidence of motivation and even of events so meager and fragmentary, though Thorndike has been far more generous to posterity in this regard than his contemporary William Gray of Salem whose name was frequently coupled with his own.

A debt of gratitude is due to the many who have helped to provide the scattered pieces of the Thorndike story that they might be assembled in an orderly account. Mr. Robert H. Haynes and his staff at the Harvard College Library, Miss Alice G. Lapham, formerly curator of the Beverly Historical Society, Mr. Robert W. Lovett of the Manuscript Division of the Baker Library of the Harvard University Graduate School of Business Administration, Mr. Stewart Mitchell and his associates at the Massachusetts Historical Society, and Mr. Walter Muir Whitehill of the Boston Athenaeum, have been particularly generous of their time and energies.

Grateful acknowledgment is made of the interest and thoughtfulness of the Honorable William Phillips, President, and Mr. A. H. Webber, Secretary, of the Beverly Historical Society.

The three men without whose encouragement this study could never have been carried out are Mr. Arthur H. Cole, Professor of Business Economics and Librarian of the Baker Library of the Harvard University Graduate School of Business Administration, Mr. Clifford K. Shipton, Librarian of the American Antiquarian Society and Harvard Archivist, and Mr. R. Amory Thorndike, direct descendant of Israel Thorndike.

Because of Israel Thorndike's part in the opening to settlement of the Western Reserve of Connecticut it is appropriate to note that this study of his life is appearing in the year of the one hundred and fiftieth anniversary of Ohio's admission to statehood and is included in the Ohio Sesquicentennial List of Books.   J. D. F.

Acknowledgments

The author is indebted to the following for permission to quote from copyrighted works:

To the American Council of Learned Societies for permission to quote from the entry on Israel Thorndike by Sidney Gunn in the *Dictionary of American Biography*, published by Charles Scribner's Sons.

To Appleton-Century-Crofts, Inc., for permission to quote from Thomas Bridgman, *The Pilgrims of Boston and Their Descendants* (1856), and J. B. McMaster, *A History of the People of the United States from the Revolution to the Civil War* (1885-1913), Volume IV.

To the Colonial Society of Massachusetts for permission to quote from Dr. Octavius Thorndike Howe, "Beverly Privateers in the American Revolution," from the *Transactions* of the Society for 1920-1922 published in Volume 24 of the *Publications of the Colonial Society of Massachusetts*.

To the Essex Institute for permission to quote from *The Diary of William Bentley, D.D., Pastor of the East Church, Salem, Massachusetts,* (1905–1914) and the following items in the *Essex Institute Historical Collections:* "The Reminiscences of Robert Rantoul," Volume 6 (1864), and Robert S. Rantoul, "The Essex Junto—the Long Embargo—and the great Topsfield Caucus of 1808," Volume 19 (1882).

To Houghton Mifflin Company for permission to quote from Lucy Larcom, *A New England Girlhood* (1890) and the *Life, Letters and Journals of George Ticknor* (1909).

To Little, Brown and Company for permission to quote from Henry Cabot Lodge, *Life and Letters of George Cabot* (1878) and *The Private Correspondence of Daniel Webster,* Fletcher Webster, editor, (1857).

To the Princeton University Press for permission to quote from C. R. Brown, *The Northern Confederacy According to the Plans of the "Essex Junto", 1796–1814,* (1915).

Contents

List of Illustrations

Israel Thorndike,
Federalist Financier

ONE

The Young Thorndike

ORIGINS AND EARLY LIFE

The winter of 1761 was marked by storms which raged up and down the Atlantic coast of North America lashing the sea into uncontrollable fury. Great mountains of green and boiling white water hurled themselves against the rocks and headlands and beat upon the small sailing craft that were so presumptuous as to defy the gales or so unfortunate as to be caught out in them. On board one such vessel, bound from Philadelphia to the port of Beverly, Massachusetts, was a mariner named Andrew Thorndike.

Waiting for Andrew on the family farm in Beverly were his wife Anna, five months pregnant with twin daughters, and their four children of whom the youngest, Israel, was six years old. Anna and her brood were doing more than merely waiting for the home-coming of their husband and father. There were the usual winter chores to do about the farm, the stock to feed and care for, the fire to be tended. Like so many families along the coast, the Thorndikes combined farming with seafaring to earn a livelihood.

At length word came about Andrew. His ship had foundered in a storm and he had been lost at sea. It cannot be supposed that any hope was held out for Andrew's ultimate appearance, but it was four years before he was declared legally dead and his estate admitted to probate. Meanwhile the family continued to work the farm. The farm comprised a half-house, a barn, and several parcels of tillage, pasture and woodlot. The whole was valued at £168/05/00 and automatically went to Joseph, the eldest son, under the laws of primogeniture prevailing in the British colony.

Young Israel's share of his father's estate was very modest. In 1773, when the estate was finally cleared up, Probate Judge Benjamin Lynde set aside the sum of six pounds from Andrew's personal estate to pay for Israel's board for the next two years, until he should become twenty years of age, but after the allowed deductions of £102/19/2 had been subtracted from the total personalty of £113/18/00, there remained only £10/18/10. The widow received a third and the balance was divided among the four older children and the posthumous twins Anna and Mary. Each child received one pound and four shillings. This was the amount of Israel Thorndike's patrimony.

Who were these Thorndikes and how did they happen to be living in Beverly, in the colony of Massachusetts Bay, when tragedy struck their home in the year 1761?

The children of Andrew Thorndike, and that includes Israel, as we have seen, were of the fifth generation of the family to live in Essex County. Their immigrant ancestor was a certain John Thorndike who came from England to Boston; from Boston he went to Ipswich in the year 1633 as one of the original twelve proprietors of that settlement.

Unlike most of the earlier settlers of the Massachusetts Bay Colony, John Thorndike came from a family with some education and a bit of property. The genealogies tell of a brother in holy orders. There is also some mention of estates in Lincolnshire, but given the size of the Thorndike families and the inheritance laws, it is doubtful that John Thorndike was any better off than the ordinary settler of solid yeoman stock. The more prosperous neighbors of these stalwarts certainly had less reason to risk the leap into the unknown.

John Thorndike had a number of daughters and one son, Paul, after whom a promontory, Paul's Head, was named; it is still called that in Beverly. In 1668 this Paul married, and his wife, Mary Patch, bore him three sons. The second son, Paul Thorndike, Jr., born April 17, 1677, had a family of ten sons; one of these was Andrew, born November 12, 1719. Our Israel Thorndike was the son of Andrew and Anna Morgan Thorndike. He was born in Beverly on April 30, 1755.

Whatever their earlier heritage, the Thorndikes had become indistinguishable from the other small farmers of Essex County in their mode of life by Israel's time. But it was to be Israel's driving urge to change that situation and make the name of Thorndike one to reckon with, not just in Beverly or Essex County, but in the metropolis of Boston and even farther abroad.

Stone's *History of Beverly* (1843) notes that Israel, "had in youth no advantages of education except those which the public schools of his native town afforded." An earlier account in *Hunt's Merchants' Magazine* states that he was early apprenticed to a cooper and adds: "but his enterprise burst out while he was quite young."

Indeed, it burst out with considerable vigor, for by 1772, when Israel Thorndike was only seventeen years old, he was the proprietor of a very fair shipping business. Dr. Octavius Thorndike Howe says, in his "Beverly Privateers in the American Revolution," that in that year, on the eve of the Revolution, he owned six and three-eighths vessels in the fishing trade amounting to a total of one hundred and fifty tons and a value of nine hundred pounds and, in addition, operated in international trade two small craft with a combined capacity of one hundred tons and a valuation of six hundred pounds. These figures placed young Thorndike among the two largest owners in each category.

In that same year 1772, Moses Brown of Waltham (who should not be confounded with Moses Brown of Providence, Rhode Island, or with Moses Brown of Newburyport, Massachusetts) took up residence in Beverly. This was an event of some significance to Israel Thorndike, because shortly afterwards the two entered into a business partnership which was to last until 1800, when the older man retired. The mercantile firm of Brown & Thorndike was second in volume of business in Beverly, just before the Revolution, only to the importing concern of J. & A. Cabot. Brown & Thorndike specialized in two lines of merchandise: broadcloths, velvets and dress goods; and the more homely fishermen's supplies.

While his business affairs were thus flourishing, Thorndike was stricken with one of the epidemics so prevalent in the unsanitary eighteenth century. The minutes of the meeting of the Beverly selectmen held March 14, 1774, contain the item: "Ordered the Treasurer to pay Noah Creesy Six Shillings and three Pence abatement of Israel Thorndikes head Tax he being at Exstrodinary Charge in haveing the Small Pox at Boston at the Province Hospital."

Beverly inhabitants did not regard the smallpox lightly, and Hurd's *History of Essex County* (1888) tells how a few years after Thorndike's attack of the disease they threw up barricades across the roads into the town to keep out infected strangers.

On October 16, 1774, Thorndike's partner Moses Brown married Elizabeth Trask, daughter of Osman Trask of Beverly. Three years later, on October 9, 1777, Israel married Elizabeth Trask Brown's younger sister Mercy Trask, and the two business associates thus became brothers-in-law. By this time, however, stirring events on the international scene had disrupted the affairs of Brown & Thorndike, merchant shipowners.

THE REVOLUTIONARY WAR

The opening of hostilities between the British North American colonies and the mother country found the rebels lacking a navy. A first approximation to such a force began to be developed in the fall of 1775 with the licensing of privateers by the national and state governments. These vessels of prey set forth on semi-piratical voyages to seize British merchantmen and bring them in to admiralty prize courts for libeling and sale at auction, with the distribution of the proceeds among the owners and crews.

Letters of marque were also granted to ships on regular commercial cruises, authorizing them to capture enemy vessels whenever and wherever found. The Massachusetts legislature went still farther in the defense of its own coast and coastal waters by creating an official state navy.

Israel Thorndike participated in these maritime operations in several roles. He served actively as the commanding officer of a series of privateers and letter-of-marque vessels. For a part of the year 1777 he was an officer in the Massachusetts State Navy. Throughout the entire Revolutionary War period he was owner and part owner of a number of privateering ships. Thorndike's first privateering command was the schooner *Warren*, a craft of fifty tons belonging to a syndicate headed by Josiah Batchelder, Jr., of Beverly. Her armanent consisted of six guns mounted on gun carriages and ten swivel guns of lighter caliber. She carried a complement of fifty men. Thorndike sailed with the *Warren* in the fall of 1776. The owners' petition requesting confirmation of Thorndike's appointment was granted by the Massachusetts Council on October 30 of that year. In accordance with law, the *Warren* was bonded in the amount of $5,000 as a guarantee against illegal seizure or other unlawful acts by the vessel. Thorndike remained in command until the spring of 1777, when he was replaced by the first officer, Nicholas Ogleby.

Israel Thorndike was commissioned an officer in the Massachusetts State Navy on March 10, 1777. On that date he was appointed first lieutenant of the brigantine *Tyrannicide,* under the command of the hard-bitten, hard-driving Captain Jonathan Harraden. He was discharged on the following August 31. It was upon his return from this tour of duty in state service that he married Mercy Trask. At the time of his marriage Israel was twenty-two and his bride just short of twenty-one years of age.

A scant month after his wedding Thorndike was named master of the privateer schooner *Scorpion* and once more went to sea. The *Scorpion* had the same tonnage as the *Warren,* but carried only forty men on board, two carriage guns and fourteen swivels. The petition of November 7, 1777, to the council, asking for authority to commission the officers, was signed by Joseph White and Miles Greenwood of Salem, but Octavius Thorndike Howe says that Batchelder and Thorndike, both Beverly men, were major owners. Thorndike did not participate actively in the naval warfare of the year 1778, although he owned shares in several privateering ventures.

On July 8, 1778, precisely three months before their first wedding anniversary, a daughter, Elizabeth, was born to Israel and Mercy Thorndike. Elizabeth was the first of two children of this marriage, and the only one to reach maturity. She was to become the wife of Ebenezer Francis, long a friend and business associate of her father.

The year 1779 was one of ill omen for Thorndike's investments in private armed vessels. He and his partner Moses Brown were among the owners of the ship *Black Prince* and the brigantine *Defense* which were pressed into state government service against the British in the foolhardy Penobscot Expedition. The *Black Prince* was a splendid vessel from the yards of William Swett of Salisbury, Massachusetts, 200 tons, carrying eighteen guns and one hundred thirty men. She had been commissioned in the summer of 1778 and had enjoyed a fairly successful season of privateering under Captain Elias Smith of Beverly. The *Defense* was a somewhat lighter craft, brigantine rigged, 170 tons, carrying sixteen six-pounders and one hundred men. In June 1779, representatives from the Massachusetts Board of War came down to Salem and requested that the *Black Prince* and other vessels join in the contemplated attack on the newly established British base on the Maine coast. The *Black Prince*'s last cruise, under Captain Nathaniel West, had been a failure, so the owners reluctantly consented to let her join the fleet. On July 6 Moses Brown signed an indenture with the Massachusetts Board of War on behalf of himself and the other owners of the *Defense,* committing that vessel to the expedition likewise.

The best account of the ill fated Penobscot adventure is that of Walter S. Hayward in the collection of essays published as a *Festschrift* for the late Wilbur Cortez Abbott. From this

Portrait of Israel Thorndike as a young man
*(From the miniature by an unknown painter;
in the Beverly Historical Society)*

narrative it is clear that a number of factors contributed to the failure of the expedition, including the incompetent leadership of Dudley Saltonstall, the poor morale of the impressed seamen and the jealousy of the state towards the Continental Navy. But prominent among the causes of collapse was the indifference of the privateersmen to the whole enterprise. They were interested in taking prizes and making money, not in naval operations and the future of the republic. They wanted to get the business over with as soon as possible and get on with privateering. The ship *Black Prince* contributed to the panic that turned the expedition into a confused rout by mid-August. In the end both the *Black Prince* and the *Defense* were beached and set on fire by their own crews to keep them out of the hands of the British. The enemy was not dislodged from his position, the Massachusetts Navy was hopelessly discredited and the commonwealth itself was very nearly bankrupted.

Howe writes that on September 20, 1799, Brown & Thorndike petitioned the state council to grant them thirty-two six-pound cannons "to enable them to cruise against the enemies of the United States." They went on to state that they, "part owners of the armed ship *Black Prince* and the brigantine *Defense*, did agree to fit out said ship and brigantine for the expedition against Penobscot and had the misfortune to have them destroyed while in the service of the State, which misfortune has deprived them of by far the greatest part of their interest and renders them unable to carry on their business in navigation unless their contract with the Board of War be carried out." This last amounted to a request for the state to make good on the insurance which it had agreed to carry on the vessels.

In the summer of 1780, Thorndike went to sea again, this time as master of the letter-of-marque ship *Resource*, 178 tons, sixteen guns, with a crew of thirty. The principal owners of the vessel were Thorndike himself, his partner Moses Brown, Thomas Woodberry and Ebenezer Parsons. Thorndike made one voyage as captain and then relinquished the command to Richard Ober, who had the bad luck to be seized by a British sloop-of-war and carried into Jamaica. The most interesting

fact connected with the *Resource* episode to one seeking to recon-
struct the life and career of Israel Thorndike of Beverly is the
description of the man provided in the roster of the officers and
crew. From this comes our first indication of how Israel appeared
as a young man. The list is dated June 21, 1780. The Thorndike
entry reads: "age 25 yrs., stature 5 ft. 7½ in.; complexion, dark;
residence, Beverly." From the documents relating to the *Resource*
we also learn how the prize money was divided among the men
who sailed the ship. The portion of the prize money reserved
for officers and crewmen was divided into forty-two parts; the
captain, Israel Thorndike, received eight and the two mates
four parts apiece, while the remainder was distributed among
the crew on the basis of rank.

Thorndike's business papers for the month of May 1781 are
filled with memoranda and bills relating to the outfitting of
the ship *Scourge*. While the vessel was building at Salisbury,
Thorndike engaged Isaac Randall as his agent to purchase
the stores for a voyage and fifteen hundred bricks from a local
dealer for ballast. The *Scourge* was a vessel of 240 tons, carrying
twenty guns and a crew of one hundred and twenty. Timothy
Parker of Norwich, Connecticut, was commissioned master on
May 24, 1781, and three weeks later put to sea. The *Scourge*
cruised in Caribbean waters. She carried several prizes into the
French island of Martinique, and the brig *Neptune* and the sloop
Crawford into Beverly. Her luck held for only a year; on April
22, 1782, she herself was captured by the British and condemned
at Barbados.

The last venture of Brown & Thorndike in privateering during the Revolution was undertaken in the final year of the war.
On February 26, 1783, James Lovett was made captain of the
ship *Shaker,* newly purchased from J. & A. Cabot. The *Shaker*
was a converted galley, one of the very few vessels of the essentially Mediterranean type to be employed in Massachusetts.

The partners do not appear to have made a fortune out
of private armed ships, but neither did they join that large
group of shipowners who lost everything in this risky business.

The privateering era ended on a note of personal tragedy

for Israel Thorndike. On October 20, 1783, his wife Mercy Trask Thorndike died, leaving him with little Elizabeth, now five years old. Here began the repetition of that story so familiar to anyone who has examined the typical New England church-yard of a century and a half ago. There lies the husband under his slate headstone, and near him are his several successive wives, "amiable consorts" according to their epitaphs, the victims of excessive child-bearing, overwork and primitive midwifery. About them lie the smaller stones of the children who died in infancy. Israel Thorndike was to have three wives. His first bore him a son and a daughter, but only the latter survived. His second bore him twelve offspring, of whom nine reached maturity. The third was the wife of his declining years.

THE NEWBORN REPUBLIC

The end of the Revolution found the shipowners of Beverly and indeed of all Massachusetts in a parlous state. Independence from England meant separation from British markets. Lost to the new nation was the British West Indies trade, with its outlet for New England fishery and forest products. Lost to the New England merchants and carriers was the bulk of their stock-in-trade of West Indian rum and sugar for transshipment in the coastwise and European business.

Israel Thorndike was first and foremost a merchant ship-owner as long as there was profit to be gained from maritime trade. But like the other enterprising shipowners of Beverly, he had his eyes opened by the post-Revolutionary depression, and thereafter was never without investments ashore. In the summer of 1787 a group of Essex County businessmen got together to build a toll bridge across the narrow straits between Beverly and Salem to replace the ferry with its six-horse scows noted by the French traveler de Chastellux in 1782. On November 17 the Proprietors of Essex Bridge were duly incorporated by the state legislature. Named as proprietors were Israel Thorndike, George and John Cabot of Beverly, and J. Fiske and Joseph White of Salem. This was an early one of a series of toll bridges incor-porated during the period when Massachusetts began to look inward as well as out to blue horizons. A year later, at the town meeting of May 1788, Thorndike became even more closely associated with the project when he was appointed to a committee to represent the town of Beverly in connection with the bridge then being built "a crost the river."

A complication in New England affairs in this time of general economic slump was the pressing political issue of the Federal Constitution. The Massachusetts Constitutional Convention was scheduled to open in Boston in January 1788. Beverly chose to send George Cabot, Joseph Wood and Israel Thorndike as its delegates. Massachusetts was split wide open on the question of ratification. The propertied mercantile and maritime interests of the coastal area were solidly Federalist and supported ratification. The upstate agricultural constituencies were dead against it.

Israel Thorndike was a Federalist in politics. He began as a Federalist in the true and original sense: one who favored a strong central government as a guarantee of order and economic stability after the uncertainties of the Confederation. A minimum of the aspirations and desires of this group was written into the Constitution which they saw accepted and made the backbone of the new government. The Federalists distrusted popular government, and around this issue party politics emerged in the new nation. The Federalists became the formal party of that name after 1791 under the leadership of Alexander Hamilton and John Adams. They were opposed by the Republicans, subsequently labeled the Democrats, the party of Jefferson, Madison and Gallatin. In a manner quite consistent with their views on popular rule, the two parties were divided in their attitudes toward Great Britain and France. The Federalists favored British conservatism; the Republicans endorsed the French Revolution.

At the opening of the Massachusetts convention the anti-ratification forces were in the stronger position, but the Federalists gradually wore down the opposition and won the day by the narrow vote of 187 to 168. Undoubtedly the pro-Constitution forces were helped by the unrest that had culminated in Shays' uprising of the previous year, and the need felt consequently for a strong central government to maintain civil order, but old-fashioned politicking played a considerable part in the victory for ratification. Of Israel Thorndike's role in this process it was said: "He was as efficient as any man in that body; not that he made long and learned speeches, but that he talked with the yeomanry of that body in a style of common sense which they understood, and his arguments had the desired effect." We can see his short, swart figure as he buttonholed the delegates one at a time or approached them as they gathered in groups between the sittings of the convention in the stately Brattle Street Church, or when he rose briefly in meeting to make some point clear.

This passage from *Hunt's Merchants' Magazine* reveals Thorndike's method of operating in legislative or quasi-legislative bodies. It is disappointing, when one looks at the records of several such gatherings, to find no account of oratorical outbursts by the man, but apparently he did his most effective work in the cloakrooms and in informal conversations. Thorndike was present at the voting in the Massachusetts Constitutional Convention, and his "yea" is recorded.

In recognition of his services at the constitutional convention, Thorndike was elected to the lower house of the Massachusetts General Court, the state legislative body, by the citizens of Beverly assembled in town meeting on May 13, 1788. Possibly these same public services account for his election to the humbler office of hogreeve three days earlier!

The *Journals* of the Massachusetts House of Representatives do not reveal Israel Thorndike as a leader in the legislative deliberations of that chamber. During his first year in the house he voted unsuccessfully to have the pay of members of the state council cut from six to five shillings, and he was appointed to a six-man committee to settle the claims of the Plymouth Company to certain lands in the District of Maine. This was probably his first introduction to the possibilities of opening up that area to settlement, though it could hardly have been foreseen that he was to invest heavily and unsuccessfully in Maine lands some years later. While Thorndike sat in the legislature, a group of Beverly men, including the Cabots and Thorndike himself, submitted their petition to incorporate the Beverly Cotton Manufactury. The petition was submitted June 6, 1788, and granted the following February 3d. The founding of the Beverly concern was the earliest attempt to establish the textile industry in the United States, and signaled the coming of the Industrial Revolution to the New World. This venture grew out of that economic soul-searching which came with the postwar commercial depression, but it did not prove success-ful and was eventually abandoned.

One thinks of Israel Thorndike as primarily concerned with maritime affairs, and so he was at this time and for many years to come, until these earliest indications of a continental economic destiny for New England had become much stronger. In view of this close association of the man with the sea, we may well ask with Allan Forbes, in the State Street Trust Com-pany monograph on Thorndike's son-in-law Ebenezer Francis, the question implied in the statement: "No one has been able to enlighten the writer as to why he was known as Colonel instead of Captain." The fact is that after completing his tour of duty with the Massachusetts Navy, Thorndike joined the militia of that state and became Colonel of the Fourth Regiment of the First Brigade of the Second Division. He saw no military action and served for only a brief time, but the title Colonel clung to him all the rest of his life. By the spring of 1792 he had lost inter-est in this military role. He wrote Brigadier General Stephen Abbott from Beverly on April 24, 1792: "My private Avocations are Such that makes it inconvenient for me to hold my Com-mission." Civic duties continued to make demands upon his time, however, and the following month, at the regular May meeting of the Beverly voters, he was chosen one of forty-eight jurors on the panel of the state supreme court.

Meanwhile word about Israel Thorndike was beginning to spread beyond the reaches of Essex County and the Boston State House. The kind of impression he made on contemporaries is shown by the letter written by Tobias Lear, private secretary to George Washington, in reply to a communication from William

Prescott. On June 10, 1792, Lear wrote: "From your recommendation of that gentleman, as well as from what I had an opportunity of observing myself, I am persuaded he is a man of great worth, and one of those to whom I should have felt happy to have shown more than common civilities."

TWO

Maritime Trade

Like the course of the trade itself, the record of Thorndike's undertakings during the first few years after the close of the Revolutionary War is spotty and unsatisfactory. The Custom House bonds on file at the Beverly Historical Society show that during the years 1785–1789 Thorndike's interest was fairly evenly divided between the foreign trade and the domestic activities of fishing and coastwise carrying. With 1789 we enter the better documented period covered by the Ship Registers of the Customs District of Salem and Beverly. There is no rapid burgeoning of ship ownership to be noted, although the individual firm of Brown & Thorndike emerged dramatically from its position as owners of a fleet of sixty- and seventy-ton schooners to become the proud proprietors of a full-rigged ship, the *Fabens*, of 243 tons, built at Salisbury, Massachusetts, and purchased new by the partners late in 1789.

As more evidence accumulates, a clearly discernible pattern of the volume and direction of Thorndike's mercantile ventures emerges. The *Nicholas Thorndike Papers* at the Beverly Historical Society pick up the story in 1789 and carry it haltingly down to 1805. More satisfactory are the *Returns of Sea Letters* for Salem-Beverly for a brief period between 1793 and 1795, followed by the clearance and occasional passport records dating from 1795 to the middle of 1801. All of these items have been removed to the National Archives. An even fuller source becomes available as the *Israel Thorndike Papers,* in the Graduate School of Business Administration at Harvard University, increase in comprehensiveness after 1799 and remain fairly substantial through the Embargo year 1807.

The bulk of Thorndike's business for more than a decade after the close of the Revolutionary War was carried on with the Caribbean area. He engaged his kinsman Nicholas Thorndike to command the schooner *Two Friends* on what was very nearly a regular run between Beverly and the West Indies. His schooner *Hope,* with Tarbox Moulton as its master, plied the same route, year in and year out, from this time down until 1800. This continuity is significant in an age when all vessels were tramps and each voyage a separate "adventure."

The usual cargoes in the West Indies trade were, on the outbound runs, provisions and manufactured consumers' goods for the planters and their slave laborers. An ordinary manifest might list such items as dried fish, beef, soap, candles, flour, gin, tow cloth and lumber. There might be added wine, shook (wood cut to size for boxes and cooperage), hoops, "oyl," glassware, shoes and "hatts." The inbound staples were sugar and sugar products, molasses and rum, and coffee.

But the cargoes were not always so routine and standardized. The *Nicholas Thorndike Papers* provide the details of a flyer in quite a different sort of commerce. On October 4, 1791, Brown & Thorndike, owners, gave sailing orders to Nicholas Thorndike, master, as follows:

> ". . . youl. proceed to Cape Francis . . . & purchas from Five to Fourteen *good negroes,* as the price may be, & lay in such food for them as is best suited to preserve their Health & proceed to the Havanna, in the Island of Cuba youl. be *Very Carefull to keep them well Secured at all times,* & on your arrival youl sell them for the most that Can be Obtained, & purchas as much Molasses as your *Vessel* will *stow."*

The transaction proceeded smoothly and according to instructions. On the last day of February 1792, Nicholas Thorndike submitted an "account current," or interim financial statement, from Cape François on the island of Hispaniola crediting his owners with the sale of his cargo of fish and provisions and debiting them with "10 prime slaves" at fifteen thousand livres together with other expenses and disbursements. Towards the end of April the schooner *Two Friends* reached the fortified port of Havana and the captain entered into negotiations with the firm of Catexa & Zavaleta for the sale of the Negroes and the purchase of a return cargo. On April 27, 1792, he sent home another account current, crediting his owners with $2,360 realized on the sale of the slaves and debiting them for the cost of "shugars" and molasses, his own commission of five per cent and a charge for a "vizet" from the doctor.

EUROPEAN COLONIAL POLICY

It was the West Indies trade that first enabled Israel Thorndike to set up in style, but not all of his Caribbean ventures prospered. Every bit as unpredictable as the perils of the deep and quite as prejudicial to profitable business operations were the vicissitudes of European colonial policy in the islands. One voyage would find American vessels welcome in a West Indies port, while on the next trip foreign merchantmen would be declared liable to seizure wherever found. This was further complicated by the state of peace or war prevailing at the time between the mother countries in Europe. It is not difficult to explain the predominance in this trade of the swiftly sailing and readily maneuverable schooner which could take flight for safety when enemies threatened.

A case in point is that of the schooner *Three Brothers*, Captain William Abbott, chartered by Israel Thorndike and George Dodge of Salem (father of the second Mrs. Thorndike) in February 1794. As was customary, the captain was handed detailed sailing and business instructions at the beginning of the voyage. The copies of these orders that remain in the *Israel Thorndike*

Papers provide a remarkably clear view of the commercial methods of the period.

Beverly 3 February 1794

CAPT. WILLIAM ABBOTT
SIR

The Schooner Three Brothers belonging to Mr. Henry Thorndike of this Town being now under Charter to us for a Voyage to the West Indies & back.

We have thought proper to appoint you to the command of her, and Our Orders are that you improve the first favourable time & proceed to Sea and make the best of your way to St. Lucia.

If it should happen on your arrival there that any part of your Cargo can be advantageously sold or bartered, You'l trade at that place either in part or entirely as you think will most serve the Interest of the Voyage, Remembering that as Cash has much the Preference in the purchase of Goods, not to engage the whole of the Cash you carry with you with your Cargo, nor to advance any untill you receive your goods and to be very cautious in giving Credit and likewise to examine carefully the Quality, weight and measure of all your goods. Otherwise you may be much imposed on either in Quality or measure.

If you should find that you cannot Trade at St. Lucia or Only in part you'l then proceed to Martinique touching at such places in that Island as you think bids the fairest for favourable sales and purchases and whenever you find any part of your Cargo can be sold to advantage or any part of your money advantageously invested you'l do it always remembering to inquire what the Duties and Charges will be before you make any engagements.

If you cannot compleat your Business at Martinique you'l then proceed to Guadeloupe touching at Dominica, or any Other of the English Islands to compleat the Sale of the Cargo. If you should still have any unsold and are sure you can have liberty to sell at the English Islands and if you should finally go to Guadeloupe it might be as well to touch at the Saints to see what may be done there.

Ifyour Business should still be unfinished you'l proceed to Basse Terre or Point Petre in Guadeloupe where you'l get the best information possible of the state of the markets at the different ports in that Island after which you'l either proceed to some other port in said Island or remain where you then are or return back to any other port you may have been at before wherever you suppose the homeward Cargo can be laid in in the best terms. You'l then proceed to load your Vessell as full as she can be stored in every point as well on the Deck as in the hold taking care to lash and secure everything on deck in the best possible manner.

We do not mean to confine you to any particular place to buy or sell neither do we mean to confine you to the purchase of any particular kind of produce for your Return Cargo, but that you should purchase such Articles as will yield the most profit at this market taking the prices subjoined to these orders for your Guide which we suppose will be the price of West India produce on your Return clear of duty taking into consideration at the same time the Investment of your whole stock and the filling your Vessel full. We suppose that with the cash and cargo you have on board allowing the Outward Cargo should sell at a tolerable advance and the Homeward Cargo should be bought as low, as we have reason to expect you will be able to purchase the following articles, to wit,

> 3800 Gallons Molasses
> 25000 lb. of clayed sugar
> 35000 lb. of Best Brown sugar
> 25000 lb. of Coffee
> 10000 lb. of Cocoa
> 4000 lb. of Cotton

which we suppose our Vessel is capable of conveying with loading her Deck full and stowing the Coffee and Cocoa in Bags, but you'l be sure to mass and store them in such manner as to keep them from the ceiling and prevent their damaging.

The foregoing being about the proportion that we should like provided the price dispatch and all other circumstances would make it appear to you best, but if you should come to bad markets or that Island produce should not be so low as we expect, you'l take more Molasses and Brown Sugar and leave out those that will pay a less Freight or otherwise to vary the proportions as you think most for our Interest.

You'l be sure to break no acts of Trade in any shape whatever, you'l likewise observe that Our Particular Orders are that you do not take on board any property or passengers belonging to any of the subjects of the powers at War; in which case there will be no pretence for any Armed Vessells detaining you but if you should be so unfortunate as to be carried into port by any armed vessel, nothwithstanding, you'll be sure to enter protest and take such legal steps as shall enable us to recover all costs and damages.

Should you die or Otherwise be incapable of commanding said Schooner through the whole of the voyage our Orders are that your Mate Mr. Mark Woodberry take the charge of the Vessell and see the foregoing Orders executed.

Probably prices of West India produce on your Return clear of Duty we suppose will be as follows, to wit—

.   .   .   .

The commission you are to charge us for the transmitting the Business of the Present Voyage is three and one third per cent for the sale of the Outward Cargo it being two thirds of 5 pr. cent & for the purchase of the homeward Cargo Two thirds of Two & a half pr. cent

per Agreement—You'l write us by every opportunity.
We are your Friends and Employers

G. DODGE
I. THORNDIKE

Beverly 5 Febr. 1794

Since writing the foregoing we have heard of the
English Fleets sailing from Europe for the West Indies,
it may therefore so happen that you can get better information and sell your cargo more advantageously at any
English Island than at a French One.

You'l therefore notwithstanding the foregoing Order
proceed directly to St. Vincents where you'l do as much
of the business of the voyage as can be done to advantage
after which you'l proceed to such other Port or Ports
as you judge best. We are your Friends, etc.

sign's

IT
GD

I acknowledge the foregoing to be a true copy of my
Orders and promise to obey them.

WILLIAM ABBOTT

The *Three Brothers* ran into bad luck just as soon as she
reached the Caribbean Sea. First she was pounced upon by a
British frigate and detained at Soufrière, on the island of
St. Lucia. Then she fell into the hands of the French and was
held in custody by a provincial Committee of Public Safety of
the Republic. Finally, on April 15, 1794, the British picked her
up again and carried her into Martinique, where the Court of
Vice Admiralty declared her a lawful prize on May 14 in
response to an impassioned plea by the King's Advocate and
Protector that she was French or, if not French, due to be de-
clared forfeit for trading with the enemy. The Yankee skipper,
William Abbott, was flexible enough in the crisis. When the
Three Brothers was auctioned off by order of the court, he

bought her back for £102/6 and carefully took a receipt. Then he notified his owners back in Beverly and continued about his business of finding a cargo for the homeward voyage.

The captain's account of the recovery of the vessel and resumption of the interrupted voyage is written in matter-of-fact, if semiliterate, prose.

St. Lucia 10 June 1794

SIR:

Our Vessels and the West India produce that they had on board when they were taken was sold at Publick Sail on the 5 of this month as I had saved the money I had on board and Living and Collected about 20 Joes of the Debts due me I have purchased the 3 brothers for 31 Joes and shall lay out the rest of my money in molasses if I can procure casks which is very Scarce Molasses is Very plenty but not to be had under 40 Sous I have Engaged 20 Hogs I shall endevour to make as much Dispatch as possible as the times are very difficult in this quarter, should I not Lay out the money I have I shall try at Martinico and so on to Leward and shall endeavor to get molasses if possible if not Lay out the money in some other produce We had the other day an account of the french fleet arriving at Guardeloopa 7 Sail of the Line and 2 frigates and a number of transports this morning a man of war sent her Boat on Shore and went Immediately to Martineco and since it is Reported that Guardeloopa is taken. But as their is so much Confusion in this place their is no noing what to believe.

In hast
WILLIAM ABBOTT

Thorndike and Dodge knew exactly what to do in this kind of situation. They had suggested as much in their initial set of orders. They collected depositions from witnesses and made up a thick dossier on the *Three Brothers* case and sent it to Thomas Dickason & Company, Thorndike's London agents, with instructions to take the case to court in England and appeal the decision of the vice-admiralty authorities in the West Indies. The partners estimated that the schooner was worth sixteen hundred dollars; the cargo, $6,234.75; and their lost anticipated net profit, three thousand dollars for half a voyage. Meanwhile Henry Thorndike, the original owner of the vessel, with whom Israel Thorndike and his father-in-law George Dodge had signed the "Charter-party of affreightment" in February, proceeded to collect from the insurance underwriter, Benjamin Pickman. His original policy had been for three hundred pounds at a premium rate of eight percent. On November 12, 1795, payment in full was acknowledged for the sum of £196/8/6. But matters did not stop there. Israel Thorndike's London associates were active in his interest and received a favorable settlement from the British courts! This meant that on April 6, 1802, the underwriter Pickman received reimbursement from Thorndike in the amount of one hundred thirty pounds.

The complexities of litigation did not interrupt the normal course of Thorndike's trade with the West Indies. That European colonial powers would be unpredictable and their local representatives capricious was an accepted fact, and the machinery was set up to deal with eventualities. The schooner *Three Brothers* returned to Beverly from her interrupted voyage and, with a minimum of turn-around time in port, set sail once more for the Caribbean.

THE SEVEN SEAS

Israel Thorndike's commercial horizons expanded enormously in 1795. Beginning in that year his ships and those in which he held an interest sailed from port to port all around the world. The incomplete clearance records for the Customs District of Salem and Beverly for 1795 provide an introduction to this story. Let us summarize a few entries:

June 26. The brigantine *Pilgrim,* Captain Osmond Thorndike, owned by Israel Thorndike and George Dodge, cleared for France laden with fish, flour, dry fish, sugar, rum, coffee, cotton, indigo and soap.

August 31. The schooner *Two Friends,* Captain Jonathan Basay, owned by Brown & Thorndike, cleared for Bilbao in Spain with 3,978 bushels of corn and twenty barrels of Indian flour.

October 28. The schooner *Hope,* Captain Tarbox Moulton, owned jointly with George Dodge, cleared for Port-au-Prince with fish, corn, hats, hoops, sheeting, coffee bags and four hundred seventy pounds of gold to the value of $4,134.

December 2. The brigantine *Fairy,* Captain Samuel Cabot, owned by Brown & Thorndike, Joseph Lee and Samuel Cabot, cleared for India with port wine, brandy, New England rum, butter, ninety-five empty bags, seven and two-third tons of iron, tobacco, porter and cheese.

December 24. The schooner *Success,* Captain Osmond Thorndike, owned by Israel Thorndike and George Dodge, cleared for the West Indies with fish, cheese, lard, soap, porter, salmon ("fish" meant codfish) and butter.

Thorndike's merchant fleet traded principally with five more or less clearly defined geographical areas. There was the American homeland, which provided the food and fishery and forest products for outward cargoes and absorbed a fair share of the imported iron, sailcloth, hemp, textiles, wines and liquors, and fine manufactured consumers' goods. A swarm of small vessels, principally schooners of shallow draught, scurried in and out of harbors and inlets all the way up and down the coast distributing foreign goods and picking up hogsheads of tobacco from Tidewater Virginia plantation landings, barrels of flour at Baltimore and aromatic pine boards from the small ports of Maine.

Thorndike's swift schooners also sailed into the Caribbean, as we have seen, and touched at the verdant islands of Guadaloupe and Nevis, at the pyramidal peak of St. Eustatia, and at Jamaica rising in a green sweep from the sea. From these places and from Martinique and Cuba and Hispaniola the vessels collected their cargoes of tropical produce.

Full-rigged ships sailed from the wharf at Beverly for the
Baltic and North Seas. From the northern ports came duck, sailcloth, hemp, iron in bars and some of the finer manufactured
goods and liquors in return for the West Indian products. England was in this North European zone, but she presented something of a special case. She took Thorndike's cargoes of raw
cotton in quantity, but in the British market he could hardly hope
to compete with Englishmen trading with their own colonial
possessions, even when this was permitted by law. England was
the center of Thorndike's financial operations. His chief agents
were Thomas Dickason & Company of London, with whom he
had close business and personal ties for the greater part of
his business life.

France and Spain and the Mediterranean ports comprised
a fourth trading area. Wines, brandies, raisins and some high-
quality textiles were purchased there. Fish was the great staple
commodity carried in exchange to these predominantly Catholic
countries, where the calendar was crowded with fast days. Next
to fish in quantity came West India sugars and coffee, and as
Thorndike's business with the Orient grew, he found profitable
Southern European markets for his China cottons and East
Indian spices.

We read of Thorndike brigs and brigantines and sometimes
full-rigged ships trading with the coastal cities of this area.
His vessels sailed up the Tagus to Lisbon or anchored off the
walled town of Cadiz and lightered their cargoes ashore. They
entered through the Pillars of Hercules, touching at Malaga,
which must have presented an unforgettable sight to the men
of Beverly as it sprawled across its plain with the hills behind
the town crowned by ruined Moorish castles, while the mountains of Andalusia provided a handsome back-drop. They stopped
at Alicante and Barcelona and proceeded to Marseilles, and
thence to Italy, to Genoa and the bustling Tuscan port of
Leghorn. Less often these merchantmen sailed on to Trieste,
the terraced port of the waning Hapsburg Empire, bristling with
fortifications, at the head of the Adriatic, or cruised still farther

east to Smyrna, threading their way through the Grecian islands, soon to be made celebrated anew by the pen of Byron.

The Orient was the last major area in Thorndike's sphere of commerce. His Indiamen visited Canton, ploughing up the Pearl River through flotillas of sampans, to carry on a restricted trade through the official guild of Chinese merchants, the *Co-hong,* in that narrow zone of commercial intercourse between the city walls and the river where the foreign "factories" existed precariously and on sufferance.

These vessels, largest and finest of his fleet, put in at the Chinese port and at Java, Sumatra and Calcutta with increasing frequency as the nineteenth century opened. China provided teas of various qualities and textiles, particularly "nankeen," a yellowish cotton cloth. India exported cottons also, and from the islands came sugar, coffee and, above all, pepper. Products that would find a ready sale in the Orient were not always easy to come by, and often the solution was to carry in casks gold bullion with which to buy the goods for which there was such a demand in the Western market.

FACTORS AND AGENTS

In every major port where he did business, both in the United States and abroad, Thorndike had strong ties with reliable local concerns that acted as his agents and undertook to sell his cargoes and provide him with goods for the return voyage. These agents also had a banking function and arranged for the handling of balances and the honoring of drafts. They were also prepared to stand by and be of all possible help in their principal's interest in the event of an emergency of any kind.

Looking at the map of Europe which doubtless hung on the wall of Israel's counting house in Beverly, and tracing the lines of his commercial activity from north to south on that map, we discover first that in St. Petersburg his agents were the firm of Brothers Blandows. Not that many of Thorndike's ships reached St. Petersburg proper. The larger ones did not attempt to navigate the shallow Neva but did their business at Cronstadt at its mouth.

Down the Baltic at Copenhagen, Messrs. Ryberg & Company accepted drafts for the financing of Thorndike's St. Petersburg business and sold at two percent commission the tobacco imported in his vessels.

Rucker & Wortmann usually handled Thorndike's affairs in the free imperial city of Hamburg on the Elbe. In the fall of 1799 they wrote that they had disposed of a consignment of coffee for him but his sugars were moving slowly. Somewhat earlier Thorndike had called upon Beeldemaker & Company of Hamburg to sell some sugar for himself, David Sears of Boston and Thomas Dickason, Jr., of London, with instructions to invest the proceeds in French silks and satins if these were available, otherwise to remit the funds to Thomas Dickason & Company.

In Bremen, the old Hansa city on the Weser, the agents were Friedrich Jacob Wuehlhausen. Goods purchased through this house in the Bremen market included "shirting linnen" and "silk hoz."

Van Staphorst & Company were Thorndike's trusted representatives at Amsterdam, where that firm not only bought and sold for his account, but also arranged to collect monies due him for insurance and performing other financial services.

Looking after his interests at the Breton port of Nantes was the house of Schweighausen & Dobrée. It was to them that he and Moses Brown wrote for legal aid in their attempt to recover $5,770 for the cargo of corn lost when the schooner *Two Friends* went down with Captain Basay and all hands at the mouth of the river Loire, below the city.

Stephen Jones, Jr., acted on behalf of Israel Thorndike and his son-in-law Ebenezer Francis at Bordeaux at the head of the Garonne's broad lower basin. In the summer of 1801, Jones was directed to sell thirty-one bales of India cloth sent him on consignment and remit the returns in specie or good bills of exchange to Dickason's in London for the partners' account.

When Thorndike was planning to send the ship *Mary*, Captain John Thissel, into the Mediterranean in the fall of 1801, he first carefully alerted his agents in the various ports of call and bade them stand ready to advise Thissel as to the state of the market and then, if the local prospects were favorable, to help him dispose of his cargo of fish and India cottons and invest the net proceeds "in the most beneficial manner." He wrote Grivegnée & Company of Malaga and incidentally told them of the dissolution of the old partnership of Brown & Thorndike, "Mr. Brown having retired from Business some time since." In this latter connection, it is interesting to note that their partnership was not an all-inclusive arrangement for Moses Brown and Israel Thorndike. While most of their ventures during their years of association were joint ones, both felt entirely free to engage in temporary business alliances with other individuals or groups.

Thorndike wrote that Captain Thissel was to call to discover if the Malaga market was *"unequivocally* better than the spannish or Italian marketts." If so, the cargo was to be sold, and the ship as well; *or,* if it was more profitable to do so, a freight might be taken on for any port; *or,* if this seemed still more advantageous, brandy might be purchased and the balance taken in Spanish bills to be remitted to Thomas Dickason & Company. At the same time he wrote to Messrs. Falconett & Company at Barcelona, instructing them to advise Thissel about market conditions in Naples and elsewhere in the Mediterranean. That very day he sent similar instructions to Webb, Holmes & Company at Leghorn. Webb, Holmes responded by writing to Captain John Thissel at Genoa, in care of Heath & Company, Thorndike's representatives in that port. While it would undoubtedly have been to their short-run advantage to sell the *Mary's* cargo on commission, they faithfully protected their principal's best interests and advised against coming to Leghorn. The sudden cessation of the Napoleonic Wars at Lunéville and Florence had combined, they said, with the arrival of a number of vessels in port to depress the price of fish.

The discouraging report from Leghorn was the very least of John Thissel's worries when he reached Genoa and dropped anchor inside the breakwater at the foot of that city's amphitheatre of sheltering hills. His agents, Heath and Company, undertook to sell the *Mary's* cargo. It was a most unsavory tale that they wrote back to Thorndike in Beverly: The agents con-

tracted with local dealers to dispose of the fish. Then it was
discovered that the quality of the fish was not up to sample.
The Genoese purchasers threatened to sue, so the stevedores were
called off the job and the unloading halted while the parties
negotiated. Heath & Company agreed to a price cut, whereupon
the unloading was resumed. The deeper the men got into the
hold of the *Mary,* the worse were the conditions they found.
There was another parley and the price was lowered again except,
as Messrs. Heath carefully pointed out in their report to Thorndike, "for what is rotten and wet by bilge water." The final
blow in this report was the observation that the India cottons
on the *Mary* were distinctly inferior to those imported by the
"English East India Company." Moreover, they alleged, the
nankeens were moth-eaten! Just how moths happened to attack
these cotton fabrics was not explained by these bearers of sorry
tidings. But even in the face of this series of unfortunate circumstances, Heath & Company could report gross sales of the *Mary's*
cargo totaling 170,035.15 Genoese livres. The final chapter of this
episode is suggested in a letter dated December 5, 1803, to Israel
Thorndike from Stembor & Roselt, his agents at the Spanish
Mediterranean port of Alicante. The members of this firm were
distressed to learn that the conduct of Captain John Thissel on
his last voyage had met with Thorndike's disapprobation and
brought about his dismissal. They hoped that the blame would
not extend to them, etc., etc. There may have been an intervening
voyage between the fish affair at Genoa and Thissel's loss of his
command, but it is certain that he emerged from the episode in
very bad odor.

THE JAY TREATY

American relations with the two major European powers were
strained almost to the breaking point during the 1790's. Since
the contacts between the new nation and England and France
were essentially maritime, this tension was naturally felt in the
New England commercial community. The sources of irritation
with England were several. British vessels waylaid and seized

American ships engaged in trade with the French West Indies. Britain was suspected of conniving to loose the Barbary pirates upon American Mediterranean shipping. Britain clung to Western frontier forts ceded at the close of the Revolutionary War and, more galling than any other acts, she continued to impress American merchant seamen on the principle "Once an Englishman, always an Englishman."

When British policy toward American trade with the French West Indies relaxed somewhat, Washington determined to make a strong bid for peace and sent Chief Justice John Jay to London to negotiate a commercial treaty. The Jay Treaty was brought back in 1795. It was not favorable to the United States, but it was felt to be better than a war, so the Senate passed it and the President signed it. In March 1796 the treaty was submitted to the House of Representatives, not because the lower house had authority to infringe upon the newly granted constitutional treaty-making powers of the Senate, but because it was necessary to implement the treaty with subsidiary legislation. The uproar over the treaty had been considerable and the debate that it precipitated in the house was vigorous. The line-up was strictly along party lines, with the Federalists favoring the treaty as an alternative to war, and the Republicans opposing the humiliating provisions and declaration of neutrality to the prejudice of their beloved France.

The threat of war if the treaty should fail of acceptance struck terror to the Atlantic seacoast towns, with their dependence upon ocean trade. Business slowed down almost to a standstill, and petitions signed by the anxious citizenry poured in upon Congress, urging the passage of enabling legislation and an end to the indecision. On April 23, 1796, the Beverly Town Meeting unanimously adopted a resolution to memorialize Congress, and Israel Thorndike and his partner Moses Brown were appointed to a committee of five to prepare the document and sign it for the citizens of Beverly praying "that provisions be made to carry into effect the Treaty between Great Britain and the United States."

Again we find evidence of the close connection between the voters and their government that existed during the early days of the republic. Thorndike's name is next mentioned in the public records of Beverly for the fall of 1798, when he and Moses Brown were chosen, doubtless to the detriment of their business affairs, to serve as petit jurors at the October term of the circuit court to be held in Boston.

INSURANCE UNDERWRITING AND THE FRENCH SPOLIATION CLAIMS

Relations between the United States and France were not bettered when the Jay Treaty was pushed through Congress with Federalist votes. As it turned out, President John Adams was able to avert the open outbreak of war between the two countries, but tension with France had become more than merely a popular emotional state. French privateering vessels roamed the seas throughout the entire period of unrest and attempted negotiation, and while a certain amount of retaliation in kind flourished, American losses at sea were very great. The experience of Israel Thorndike during the Quasi-War with France was typical of the kind of thing that was happening to his entire economic group and illustrates the impact of deteriorating French-American relations upon the maritime community. The place to look for the story of American losses is in the records of the French Spoliation Claims.

The story of the French Spoliation Claims was formerly considered the account of one of the most outrageous money grabs in the financial history of the United States, but more recent raids on the national treasury now make it appear a very minor episode indeed. An Act of Congress of January 20, 1885, gave the Court of Claims jurisdiction over claims against the Federal Government arising from the settlement of the Quasi-War with France. Of course, the claimants, the real sufferers from French privateering and naval depredations, had been dead for years, but their descendants and their descendants' attorneys insisted that in concluding the treaty with France of September 30, 1800, which was ratified July 31, 1801, the United States had abandoned claims of its nationals against the French in the amount of about twenty million dollars and therefore was morally and legally bound to assume these claims. After all, it was pointed out, the United States had received substantial and tangible benefits from the treaty, since it had obtained a release from the embarrassing provisions of the treaty of alliance with France of 1778. Claims were to be filed before January 20, 1887, on all losses attributable to attacks by French men-of-war and private armed vessels on American shipping from 1793 until the cutoff date, July 31, 1801. A total of 5,574 claims were filed, and settlement continued well into the twentieth century.

Thorndike suffered in two roles in the undeclared hostilities with France. His greatest losses were as an insurance underwriter, but vessels in which he had an interest were seized by the French, also. Thorndike customarily underwrote insurance on ships and cargoes through the Boston brokerage firm of Joseph Taylor. The Spoliation Claims documents describe in greater or less detail the loss of eleven vessels, together with their cargoes, on which Israel Thorndike was called upon to make insurance payment as fractional underwriter. There are three cases listed in which he suffered a direct loss as owner or lessee under charter. The individual accounts are vivid and read like the events of a blood-and-thunder novel even in the legal phraseology of a brief submitted to the United States Court of Claims in the 1880's. Typical were the cases of the *Eliza* and the *Ruby*. The ship *Eliza,* Captain James Odell, which was owned by Francis Amory, was bound from Boston for the Isle of Wight when she was captured on the high seas by the French privateer *Don Quichote* on February 13, 1798. Shortly thereafter she was retaken by the British ship-of-war *La Nymphe* and taken into Portsmouth, and there it was ordered that one eighth of the value of ship and cargo be paid for salvage. The cargo of coffee and sugar was insured through Taylor's office for $23,100, and so risky had the undertaking been regarded that the premium rate was eighty per cent. Thorndike's share of the assessment came to eighty-three dollars, which was refunded to his descendants by the court on January 14, 1889. The brig *Ruby,* Captain Luke Keefe, owned by James and Thomas Handasyd Perkins, George H. Apthorp and others, was picked up on about the last day of 1798 while en route from Boston to Holland. The French privateer *Bougainville* carried her into Quimper, where she was condemned as a prize, and the underwriters paid out ten thousand dollars, the full amount of the policy, plus an extra charge of 6.42 per cent for expenses. Israel Thorndike's fraction of the loss was $532.10, which was duly recovered by his heirs.

THE SHIP CYRUS AND THE EAST INDIA TRADE

On June 8, 1800, there was launched at the yards of Enos Briggs, shipbuilder of Salem, the ship *Cyrus,* an Indiaman, belonging to Israel Thorndike, William Leech, and Thomas Dickason, Jr., of London. Her length was 96 2/3 feet, her beam 26 feet 10 inches. She drew 13 feet 5 inches and her capacity was calculated at 305 tons.

Building a ship in 1800 involved the owner in more than merely the signing of a contract with a firm of shipbuilders. From the bills and memoranda in the *Israel Thorndike Papers* we find that each step of the building was a separate operation which had to be performed by a specialist, who was dealt with individually by the owner, who had to know a good deal about shipbuilding to undertake the project in the first place. Enos Briggs designed and built the hull of the *Cyrus,* and was therefore the principal contractor involved. Briggs first appears in the business records when he sent a bill on August 28, 1798, for an advance payment of three hundred dollars on the vessel he was about to build for Thorndike. In 1800 the owner received a multipage statement, minutely itemized, totaling $11,996.19. Included was an entry for $97.29 for "McIntire's Bill of Carved work &c."

McIntire could only have been Samuel McIntire, the wood-carver and architect, the ardent exponent of the delicate, sharply executed, thin classical reliefs in the Adam manner which graced the interiors of the great houses of Salem. More robust were the screaming eagles and scrollwork of the ship carving he did for the Derby and Crowninshield vessels and presumably for the *Cyrus.*

An agreement was made on February 18, 1800, whereby Thomas Fairlis undertook "to rig a vessel building by E. Briggs." The same week Samuel Hankings agreed to do joinery work on the ship and Benjamin Brown submitted a bill for hauling stores. On March 5 a receipt was signed for a "sute of spars" and three boats for the new ship. A fortnight later the poorhouse sent in its bill for oakum, which gives a hint as to how paupers were employed in Essex County in 1800.

The *Cyrus* was armed with cannon purchased for $280. Her "Roman figure head" cost $57.25; the 1466-pound anchor cost $161.26, and Paul Revere's bill for copper bolts came to $71.20. Goodwin's bill for cordage was $1,772.58. The ship's bell was purchased from Hugo Hill for $20. Bills for innumerable miscellaneous items kept pouring in to Thorndike's counting house in Beverly through the summer of 1800. Shot, cordwood, coppering, tools, hammock, hardware, water casks, tallow, "musketts," pumps, blocks, labor at $22 per month, a "trumpett," a horn lantern, an arms chest and "pistells," "349 meals of victuals," a medicine chest complete with lancets and an instrument for extracting teeth, "cyder," twelve feet of "mahogeny" for window sashes, "binacol glasses," a harpoon, cod lines, "33 tons ballast off my beach." All these comprised but a fraction of the stores, chandlery, and services that went to make up the vessel. On August 28, 1800, Thorndike summarized his outlay to date and found that his total payments came to $27,031.82½. This was very nearly the whole story. A final reckoning the following week showed that it had cost him $27,436.58 to build and fit out the ship *Cyrus.*

While the *Cyrus* was building, Thorndike had busied himself assembling a cargo to sell and a freight to carry. The value of the cargo purchased was $61,671.33½, which brought his total outlay for the venture to $89,107.92. The other partners owed him for their respective shares of this sum. Thorndike and young Dickason were equal partners, with fifteen shares each of the total of thirty-two shares. William Leech, the captain, held the remaining two shares. The value of the freight was $106,080, and Thorndike collected a commission of one per cent of this amount for his services in getting a freight together. A specific record of the nature of this last is missing from the documents relating to the voyage, but its character is suggested by two bills of lading dated July 1, 1800. Both are for specie to be invested in Calcutta. John Lowell, Jr., was credited with two kegs, two thousand dollars' worth of gold; Daniel Gilman & Co. with six kegs, six thousand dollars' worth.

The *Cyrus* was an Indiaman. Thorndike had become increasingly more interested in the East Indies trade during the closing years of the eighteenth century, and by the fall of 1801 he could write to his agents at Malaga and observe that "my Concerns being chiefly to the East Indies . . ." Several Eastern voyages by Thorndike vessels are recorded for the period just prior to the turn of the century. The *Fairy*, in which he held a share, sailed for the mountainous equatorial island of Sumatra and returned in 1796 laden with 158,807 pounds of pepper and a smaller amount of nutmeg. The brig *Pilgrim* made her way to Batavia and sailed up the waterway through the marshy plain to that steaming and humid transplanted Dutch city to take on a similar cargo in the following year. She touched at the sugar-rich volcanic speck of Mauritius in the Indian Ocean on the homeward passage.

In 1798 the ship *Mary,* wholly owned by Israel Thorndike, reported a voyage to the Bay of Bengal and up the crowded Hooghly River through the low-lying Ganges delta, past the imposing defenses of Fort William to Calcutta, almost a hundred miles from the sea. There she loaded 231,000 pounds of sugar and assorted merchandise for her owner.

Two other Thorndike ships brought home cargoes of sugar from the Indian Ocean that same year, the ship *Four Sisters* from Batavia and the ship *Sally* from Calcutta. The ship *Cyrus* was built to take her place in this trade. By the first week in July 1800, she was ready for sea. The whole undertaking of building and fitting her out had taken almost two years. At length the final step in the preparation for the voyage was taken: the owners' orders were handed to Captain Leech. These instructions were as follows:

Beverly 9th July 1800

CAPT. WILLIAM LEECH

SIR

Our Ship Cyrus which you Command being now ready for Sea, our orders to you are that you improve the first favourable time and depart from this port, and make the best of your way to Calcutta and on your arrival at that place you'l be careful to inform yourself of the best manner of doing your business, and of the Character of the people that must necessarily be employ'd by you in procuring and packing your Cargo; and after spending a few days to get the *Necessary information,* you'll proceed to purchase a return Cargo on the best terms you can of such articles as is named in the Schedule, annexed to these orders, or such as come the nearest to them that are the best suited for this Market, and such as are the Cheapest compared to their Qualities but if you should find some much dearer in proportion to their Qualities than others, in that Case you must vary the proportions, taking more of those that are the Cheapest, and leaving out a part of those that are dear, but you will recollect that it is absolutely necessary that you should have samples brought you of all such goods as you mean to buy, from many places, and from many people in order that you may raise a Competition, to enable you to get them as Cheap as possible, and after cheapening them as much as possible, and deciding on the best time to begin your purchases, you'll proceed to receive and Pack your goods, taking Care to examine them very minutely, before they are received by you, and we conceive that it will be necessary to measure the *Length, Breadth* and *Quality* of nearly every piece of goods you purchase, or at least buy so many of each Kind, and from each Person from whom you buy, as to

be sure you are not imposed on in your Purchases, it
frequently happens that many of the goods turn out
a little short in Length or Width, or that the middle
of the piece is of an inferior Quality to the Outside, it
therefore requires great Care to guard yourself against
those deceptions, and whenever detected to refuse the
goods altogether or to oblige the Seller to make such a
heavy abatement on them as to make them better than
the first Contract. Should you bring any Bandanno
Handkerchiefs, you'l recollect that they ought to be
7 yards long & 1 yard wide, and if they are short of that
and can be bought low in proportion, perhaps it will
be as well as to have them at full measure. Our particular
orders are, that you have the goods packed and screwed
as closely as possible, and also screwed into the Ship
as closely as they can without injury to the Bales or
Ship, that you Dunnage the Ship with Stone Ballast, as
much above the Keelson as to make her *perfectly safe*
for stowing *Bale goods* in the *Ground* Tier, that you
furr off in the Bilges of the Ship from the Pumps to
within 6 feet of the Foremast 4 or 5 inches from the
Ship's Ceiling, and leave a *free Water* Course in the
Crop of the Bilges, betwixt the Ceilings, that the Ship
is carefully ceil'd & furred off with Matts & Boards in
every other part, and to prevent a possibility of damage
without Shipwreck, you'l dunnage betwixt Decks, and
leave a Water Course under it & put a batten up & down
the side & Ceil light on that, so as to turn any Water
that may come through—you'l Caulk and pay your
Lower Deck, in the best & most faithful manner, and
every other seam from the Wales up inside and Out,
& be sure to leave no defect, that can admit Water.

It may so happen that on your arrival you may find
Spanish Dollars cheap, or that many goods may have
been recently bought up or Shipp'd off and none but
refuse remain in the Market, or that from some Cause
or other, you cannot have so good a choice of Goods of

the Kind you want to buy, as you may reasonably expect to have in a short time, should any of the foregoing Circumstances occur, & to so great a degree as you think would Justify your waiting a more favorable time to do your Business, you'l of Course wait a reasonable time for more favorable Circumstances, always Keeping yourself prepared to Commence and compleat your Business at the most favorable moment.

On your Outward passage you'l always keep your lower Deck Hatches off, and also your upper Deck Hatches as much as you can without endangering the Ship, and always when you can with Convenience keep a wind Sail set to force down fresh air into the Hold, and as often as once a day in good weather let in a Quantity of Sea Water, and wet the Ship with it throughout on the inside, to keep her sweet & Cool to prevent her rotting, the same may be done on the Homeward passage, so far as to let in Sea Water and pump it out again, taking Care that the Quantity is so small as not to damage the Goods. You'l be sure to oblige your people to keep themselves clean, and to keep the Ship clean, and frequently sprinkle the Births with Vinegar to prevent sickness.

On your leaving Calcutta for Home, you'l bring out at least Six Months Stores & provisions at full allowance and should you find you have more on board sell them on the best terms you can as also one of the Ships Cables & Anchors to be deliver'd the pilot Boat after you are sure you'l have no other use for it, you'l also sell such of your Ship Stores, as you think will be useless, so that the Ship may be as little encumber'd as possible, consistent with the most perfect safety of the Ship & Cargo.

You'l always keep a Man at Masthead in the daytime to look out, and run from everything you see the moment you discover them, and in taking a Pilot be careful that you dont suffer any pilot vessel to come too near you, before you have ascertained, that it is not a

Wolf in Sheeps Cloathing, from the present appearances however there appears to be such a good understanding betwixt our Commissioners in France, and the French Government, that we have nothing to fear from the Cruizers of that Nation, but if Contrary to our expectation, you should be interrupted in your Voyage by the Cruizers of any Nation whatever, you'l be careful to claim the property & enter proper protests, and take every other Legal or prudent Step to recover it with damages, and never quit the property, while you can keep possession of it, or keep it out of the hands of the Captors.

The money belonging to the Freighters, you'l invest in dry goods agreeable to their directions, taking Care that you keep the Charges appertaining to each persons Money & goods disctinct & Seperate, *and that you have a Sample Bale accompanying each persons goods, with Samples of each Quality in each Bale which must be kept clean & entire;* you'l forward from Calcutta to each Shipper duplicate Invoices & accounts Current of their respective Concerns; you'l also observe that they are to pay the Charges of their own Money & Goods, such as store Hire, Packing Duties, &c. *and also 2½ pct. for your Commission.*

Should you have time to spare, you'l make a journey to Saranpore a Danish Settlement near Calcutta and there obtain every information of all their Imports & Exports, their Customs & Charges, and whether a Cargo can be laid in there on as good or better terms than at Calcutta.

We recommend your purchasing for your return Cargo on Owners account, goods of the following description as nearly as you can, consistent with their Comparative prices and Qualities, and their suitableness for this Market Varying the proportions as Circumstances shall make it expedient, as before recited in the former part of these orders.

At this point in the captain's instructions there appears a detailed list of India cotton goods suitable for a return cargo. The orders then resume.

> Your officers & people will be entitled to the Wages & privileges set against their names in the Shipping Paper, but no one must fill the privilege of another, you are to pay Mr Ellis Three hundred Spanish Dollars in Calcutta which is to be in full for his whole Services for the Voyage. You are also to pay Mr Dix forty dollars which is to be in full for his whole Services.
>
> Your own Emoluments for Transacting the whole Business of the Voyage are to be ten dollars p. Month Wages, Five p. Cent privilege on what the Vessel *actually carries on cargo*. Twenty five hundred Dollars by way of Commissions for doing the business of the Freighters & Owners, and what the Freighters goods at 2½ p Cent of all short of paying you is to be in full for all your Commission, for Freighters & Owners property; the Ship is to pay all your necessary Shore expenses while on the Business of the Voyage; and to find you in Ship & Cabin Stores on Ship board.

Here are quoted a long list of "prices current" for East India goods on the Italian market at Leghorn.

> We thought best to give you this information, that you might be prepared to buy of those goods if you find them Cheap.
>
> Should you by Death or otherwise be rendered incapable of Commanding the Ship Cyrus through the whole of the Voyage Our orders are that your Chief Mate take the Charge of the said Ship Cyrus, and that he jointly with Mr Phineas Ellis take the Charge of the Cargo & govern themselves by the foregoing orders.
>
> You'l write us by every Opportunity, even by way of England directed to the Care of Messrs. Thomas Dickason & Co.

On you appearing off Cape Ann on your return
hoist as a Signal a White Flag at your Maintop Gallant
Masthead and an American Jack at your Fore & a
Tarpoling at the Foretopsail yard arm, & the one that
shall be the most Conspicuous from the Shore and when
up with the Light House fire a Gun, wishing you a safe
& prosperous Voyage

We are

> Your Friends & Employers
> ISRAEL THORNDIKE
> WM SHIMMIN *for* THOMAS DICKASON, JR.
> WILLIAM LEECH

I acknowledge the Foregoing to be a true Copy of
Orders which I have received from the Owners of the
Ship Cyrus which I promise to comply with

> WILLIAM LEECH

While the ship *Cyrus* was on her maiden voyage to Calcutta,
Thorndike was engaged in other ventures in Eastern waters.
Early in 1801 the ship *Sally* returned from Batavia, and the
brigantine *Rambler* from Calcutta. During the same period
Thorndike entered into a series of business arrangements with
David Sears of Boston for further exploiting the profitable East
Indian trade. Sears, the younger Dickason, and Thorndike
had been associated two years before, in 1799, when they
traded in sugar on the Hamburg market. On the previous occasion Thorndike had been the major shareholder; this time
Sears put in the larger sum. Sears and Thorndike outfitted the
ships *Borneo, Arab* and *Ganges* in 1801 at a total cost in excess
of $160,000. The names of the vessels reflect the trade for which
they were intended.

The *Cyrus* returned from India in July 1801, just a year
after she sailed out of Beverly harbor. From the sales of cotton
goods imported from Calcutta there was credited to Israel
Thorndike's account the sum of $24,418.90. It was decided to
send the ship to the Mediterranean late in the summer with a

cargo of East Indian goods, and Thomas Dickason & Company was instructed to advise Captain Leech what freights he should take from that area to Northern Europe.

Young Dickason visited Boston that fall, and Thorndike's letter to him, written the day after his return to London gives an illuminating summary of certain aspects of Thorndike's trading problems.

Beverly 8th Novr. 1801

8 pm

My Dear Sir

I presume that the fine westerly wind of this pleasant day has boarn you so far as to leave the American shore quite out of your view. Haveing had the pleasure of seeing & converseing with you but yesterday, I can have no new Idea to offer on business, but to Committ to writing what was then agreed on, as it stands in my mind, which was as respects the Cyrus, that if she should go to England or any neighboring port where you could controul her, that you take on yourself to send her on any voyage that you think the most beneficial for the present Owners giveing preference to a Voyage to the East Indies, and if her stock should be large Either as owners property or on freight, or Share, then of Course Calcutta, Manilla, or Canton must be the object, but if small Sumatra for Pepper or Gogo for Cotton. the America arrived at Salem from the *North Coast* of Sumatra a few days since with about 900,000 lb. of Pepper which was bot at 6 cents pr. pound. You will before this reaches you have heard from Andrew Thorndike & know what he is doeing & what the prospects are & will of course know the best thing that can be adopted under the circumstances, but let me pray you to order the Cyrus as you think best the same as though the property was your own, should she come here I shall be governed by Messrs. Sears & Shimmings opinion what to do with her.

As to the Arab Ganges & Eliza, I conceive the Understanding to be that those ships or any other that may be thought necessary to employ under the direction of Mr. Andrew Thorndike, are to be employed for account & Risk of the *present Owners* of those *three ships,* and as it is probable that one or more of them will be in England early next winter, I think you had better send them to the best Marketts for the sale of their Cargoes (which will probably be Holland if Tea) & Copper them if you think best & send them out to India again as Soon as possible, or Should you git such Information as you think it adviseable to Purchas freight or Charter any vessel or vessels for the same concern I think it had better be done in the Name of Mr. Sears & myself & I hereby ingage to take the same proportion as I hold in the Arab Ganges & Eliza, on the Other hand such we hear from A. Thorndike & our advices are Such as to justify our sending out to him more Tonnage we shall do it for the same concern.

—hopeing that this will find you and your family safely arrived & enjoying your friends in England, I am with Sincere

Esteem your Friend
I. T.

Indicated here are the concern of the partners in the wishes of their colleagues and the peculiar role played by the supercargo. Thorndike did not often use a supercargo, preferring to entrust his captains with the business management of his enterprises. He did his best to interest his nephew, Andrew Thorndike, in remaining in the field as his confidential personal representative, but after a year or two young Andrew resolved to return home and enter retail trade. In this instance the younger Thorndike was in charge of the purchase of cargoes for three vessels in such remote areas that he could seek no outside advice. In the sale of these goods in Western ports this responsibility could be shared with agents.

Thorndike wrote to Dickason again while the *Cyrus, Ganges, Arab* and *Eliza* were in Southern waters. In a letter dated Beverly, December 3, 1801, he suggested several alternate courses to follow.

By the Regulus which arrived from Calcutta a few days since, we are inform'd of the arrival of the Ganges at Bombay we have heard nothing further from the Arab from which I presume she has gone from Gogo to Canton or London in which case both those ships & perhaps the Eliza will be with you in England before they return to this country should that be the case youl send them back for Cotton on acct. of present owners if you think best but if that plan should not promise a *good profit* & you should think it for the Interest of the Concern to abandon it, it is Mr. Sears wish as well as mine that the Ships should be *sold* in *Europe* for the most they will fetch, & you will of course send them to France or spain for sale, or sell them in London as may appear the most advantageous at the time at any rate if the ships will sell at tolerable prices they had better be sold in Europe & replaced here where they will be very cheap.

Very shortly after posting this letter Thorndike received word of the negotiations in progress for a European peace. On Christmas Day, 1801, he wrote to Captain Leech of the *Cyrus,* by way of a Mediterranean correspondent, with new orders dictated by the turn of political events.

Peace having taken Place I have made up my mind for a great *sacrafice* on the Cyrus & her Cargo but I console myself in the belief that you will do everything in your Power to make the loss fall as light as possible.

I am now more than ever impressed with the Idea that money will be *constantly growing better* both hear & in Europe & of course that the trade generally will leave a loss to those who pursue it, therefore I should Vastly prefer having the Cyrus sold in Europe if a tolerable price could be obtained for her & the Proceeds of her and her cargo could be placed in London or Elsewhere in *perfect safety* and without much loss.

Time passed very slowly in the days of sailing ships. Not until we reach the correspondence of the late spring do we get any indication of how these ventures turned out. Thorndike wrote Dickason on May 7, 1802, after the Peace of Amiens had been in force for two months.

I see we must do badly with the cotton pr. the Ganges, this is a Misfortune that we could not foresee & for which we ought not to reflect on ourselves, because our Cotton plan taken togeather has succeeded better than we had a right to Expect, so far as respects our gitting through without any Embarrassment, and the alteration of times that has taken place which so materially lessons our profits is a thing that no human being could foresee or prevent.

I have the pleasure to inform you that the Arab arrived at Boston yesterday noon & had the remarkably short passage—120 days. All well excepting Danl. Heard ye. Supercargo who died at Canton. The Merchant who bot the Cargo at Canton fail'd which detained the ship there much longer than was Expected & was the means of Bryants being obliged to vary the cargo from the Original schedule sent you some time since, but fortunately no loss.

.   .   .   .

We are all at a great loss to determine whether to unlade the Ship here or to send her to Europe but shall make up our minds in a few days, it rests with Mr. S [ears]. The Eliza was by advice of Mr. Cherry to leave Bombay for Sumatra ye. 28th Octr last for Cargo of Pepper she must do very *well indeed*. I Expect she will make a profit on her return cargo of $45000 at least, &

I presume that she is with you & gone to her markett before this moment. The Ganges & Eliza I hope youl sell in Europe & as we hear ships have brot great prices in Holland we hope those will also.

The story was continued three weeks later, when Israel Thorndike again reported to his friend and associate in London.

Since my last it has been determined to unlade the Arab in Boston which has been done & the Ship sold for $11,000 as she came from sea Excepting her war like implements & what little provisions was on board her. in my last I informed you that the Arab & Cargo would nett about $93,000 after paying the portage bill, I think I shall not be $2000 out in my Calculation, this is no Great thing & the Ganges will be Still worse, but we have this consolation, that if the war had continued we Should have done well.

With regard to the future of the business, Thorndike thought there might be some money in the cotton trade. With vessels of four hundred to four hundred and fifty tons

the business might be carried on to make a good *peace* profit by it say 12 to 15 pct. pr. Annum after paying insurance and all other Charges, this I suppose you would call *miserable* after what you have experienced here, but those times have past, not to return to Us, but perhaps to Our Children.

The actual receipts from the sale of the *Arab* and her cargo fell below Thorndike's estimate. A statement dated May 10, 1802, gives the gross return at $98,685.99, leaving a net of $63,776.28 after charges.

We do not learn the fate of the *Eliza,* but Thorndike's letter to Dickason of August 10, 1802, indicates what happened to the two principal ships in the East India venture.

I observe you have sold the Ganges & Cyrus the former for 10,000 & the latter for 14000 Dollars, I am *perfectly* sattisfied with the sale because I know you did what you thought best, but that of the Cyrus is truly unfortunate because the Extra expense in gitting home the Crew & the loss of the freight home will reduce her very low indeed, but A [ndrew] Thorndike tells me you sold both ships to one man & that you had sold them under such circumstances as led you to think it just to put the Ganges at $9000 & the Cyrus at $15000 I hope this is the case which would make each sale something more equal. I think the Cyrus would now fetch in Boston 17,000 to 18,000 Dollars Cash. Mr. Sears & myself bot a Ship last week of abt. 360 Tons badly found a *Cable short* had been one voyage & not sheathed for which we paid $14000 Cash down she will cost $18000 fit for Sea with wooden Sheathg.

Thus ends the saga of the ship *Cyrus,* Captain William Leech, from the advance payment to the shipwright who designed her to the grumbling over her final disposition by sale in London. There ends also any legend about Israel Thorndike's being a cold and infallible business machine or an imperturbable gambler who could take his losses without a sign of emotion.

Dickason's withdrawal from mercantile ventures when the temporary cessation of the Napoleonic struggle made them no longer highly profitable is reflected in his letter to Thorndike dated London, March 2, 1803. Dickason was ever the sprightlier correspondent.

I am already turned into the Humdrum Merchant of Londn. looking neither to the right nor to left transacting the business of our Correspondents, with incessant attention & fidelity—pray come here, & enliven the scene, *with conversation at least,* about E. I. voyages.

ALEXANDER HODGDON EIGHT DAYS FROM BEVERLY JOSIAH LOVETT MASTER BOUND TO SUMATRA

The ship *Alexander Hodgdon* after a storm at sea. She was owned by Israel Thorndike during the period when Josiah Lovett commanded her.

(From a painting in the Beverly Historical Society)

Thorndike described his own similar situation in writing to one Edward Fettyplace.

> I am much retired from business at present, & the enormous price of shipping, sailors & wages, & every thing appertaining to Navigation, almost discourages me from haveing any further concern in it, but if I could git a good vessel soon on reasonable terms I would send her around the Cape of Good Hope with a Small stock.

Actually, Thorndike was unable to keep his finger out of the East India trade, and at the very time he was selling off his ships he enlisted David Sears' participation in another Oriental adventure. Together they induced Andrew Thorndike to postpone his retirement from the business end of the trade and put him in charge of a voyage to the East Indies and China. This was the voyage of the ship *Alexander Hodgdon*, 377 tons, the vessel mentioned as having been purchased unsheathed in August 1802 for fourteen thousand dollars. She cleared for Eastern waters with sixty thousand dollars in Spanish milled dollars on board, Josiah Lovett commanding.

There is a painting of the *Alexander Hodgdon* in the Beverly Historical Society titled: ALEXANDER HODGDON EIGHT DAYS FROM BEVERLY JOSIAH LOVETT MASTER BOUND TO SUMATRA. The vessel is shown in a sorry state, apparently just after a gale. The tops of all three masts have snapped and the crew is busy disentangling the rigging and putting her back into sailing condition again. This is a tantalizing scene because we seek in vain among the Thorndike papers for mention of this dramatic episode.

THE HAPPY NEUTRAL

The reopening of the Napoleonic Wars in Europe in the spring of 1803 was the cause of solid satisfaction and considerable relief in the New England shipping community. Thorndike reacted to the good news—good in Beverly, Massachusetts, if not in count-

less homes in Britain and on the continent of Europe—with an
optimistic and most revealing letter to Thomas Dickason, Jr.

Beverly 9th Sept 1803

Thos. Dickason Jr Esqr
Dear Sir

It is a long time since I have had the pleasure of a
line from you, and now as the war betwixt your Country
& France has actually taken place, we on this side of the
Water think it will be a Considerable time before Peace
will be permanently settled again, under those Impressions our India speculations are again in Operation &
our friend Sears & myself have undertaken in some lately,
& am about extending it further, and all that is now
wanting to put it in lively opperation is your presence
& participation, & I sometimes indulge a hope that I shall
have the pleasure of seeing you in this Country again
with your family.

We have lately recv'd letters from Andrew Thorndike dated at Batavia 26th March last informing us that
the Ship Alex. Hodgdon was loaded with upwards of
600,000 D of Pepper & that he should sail the next day
for Isle de France & Europe, we were in Hopes his ship
would have been laden with Coffee in which case she
would have Called at England for advise & would have
made us a great deal more money but Coffee was very
low when she sailed & we cautioned A T against haveing
anything to do with it by which we loose 40 to 50000
Dollars, she will now stop at Cadiz for advice & will
proceed north or south as the prospects shall offer, but
at any Rate the *principle* part of the *Proceeds* of her
Cargo will be *remitted* to your House.

I am also about sending a ship to the Mediterranean
with Coffee & Calcutta goods and shall order the (principle part) of the proceeds of her Cargo remitted to your
House or to load Galipoli Oil for London, in fine the
surplus of my European Cargoes will always center in

London and it may & probably will be very Convenient for me to Open a Credit for £30,000 Sterling in London that I may draw for that sum or any part thereof at any time when I may have occasion for it, whether I have funds there or not, & pay as Interest for such time as I may have the use of the money, I therefore propose to you (individually) or to your House that you Give me written liberty to draw on you at any time for 12 months after the date of your letter for any sum that I please not exceeding £30,000 sterling more than I have specific funds appropriated to Meet. Unless you think the sum too large, in which case *name* a less sum, this will afford me a facility that will be greatly to my advantage & cannot (I think) be any injury to your House or you, for it is probable that I shall not have occasion for any advances for any great length of time, & I assure you on the word & Hon. of an honest man that you run no kind of Risk for my habits of doing business is such that I am sure you never will:—I (you know) never run so great Risk in any Bottom uninsured, or in any One speculation as to wound me very deeply if it should prove unsuccessfull, & I have lately Closed all my accounts & have a Clear unincumbered property of upward of $400,000—beside a handsome Expectation from a father in law who is far advanced in age. I am this particular to shew you that you run no risk in giveing me this Credit of which I am very desirous because it gives me a great advantage in availing myself of the highest rate of Exchange, besides the anticipation I will therefore thank you to be Explicit in your Answer on this subject.

Pray give my best respects to Mrs. Dickason & your family in which Mrs. Thorndike most Cordially joins, & believe me to be with

Great Respect Dear Sir your
Devoted friend
I. T.

This letter tells us several things about the upturn of neutral commerce with the resumption of hostilities, as well as giving further insight into Thorndike's business methods and his conscious formulation of executive policy.

The ghoulish reference to the "handsome Expectation" from his father-in-law was based upon a realistic appraisal of the facts. The Salem clergyman and diarist William Bentley recalled a few items of information about this father-in-law in a journal entry of January 23, 1814.

> The first person of distinction in Salem was Capt. G. Dodge, Merchant, who died aged 82, 18 jan. 1806, & one of the three eminent merchants, Mason, Williams & Dodge. He said he doubled his estate after 60 years of age. He was active, acute. Two d. married Cabots, Andrew & John, famed merchants of Beverly. His youngest d. married Israel Thorndike, an eminent merchant in Boston from Beverly.

When George Dodge died in 1808 (not 1806), he left an estate valued, according to the Essex County probate records, at $286,060.24. Under the terms of the will his daughter Anna Thorndike received "one full sixth part." The administrators' accounts show that in 1810 Israel Thorndike was paid slightly more than forty-five thousand dollars as his wife's share of her father's estate. Forty-five thousand dollars was a most respectable inheritance and, coupled with Thorndike's own fortune, gave strong support to the request for a substantial sterling credit.

THE RIVER PLATE AFFAIR

During the period that Israel Thorndike was expanding his Far Eastern business and then contracting it again with the coming of the temporary peace, he and David Sears and Thomas Dickason, Jr., became involved in a venture to the River Plate in South America which caused them great perturbation. Records are scanty and we come upon the story in the middle.

Two vessels, the *Sally,* Captain Taylor, and the *Five Brothers,* Captain Ellis, had been sent to the Spanish South American colonies with cargoes to sell and instructions to return with cargoes of tallow and hides.

Thorndike wrote Dickason on August 10, 1802:

> Our South American Business will turn out badly. The Government there appears determined to embarras it all in their Power & to pay little or no respect to any licenses given or agreements entered into by their predecessors alledging that they acted without authority, but I believe we Stand on as favourable ground as any vessel in Rio de Plata. The 5 Brothers has permission to land & sell her Iron & their was at that time the apperance of her being permitted to load immediately, she was however detained with the rest. Taylor on his arrival Entd. his cargo which was considered as *legally Imported,* but was afterwards stop'd in the Custom House. he has daily the assurances of its being liberated.
>
> The Sally was nearly loaded with hides & Tallow ye. 1st of June & would sale for home in 15 or 20 days, & the Consigner says to us that he Expects to have leave to load the 5 Brothers soon in which case he shall take freight, probably for *London*—should she come into your River sell her for the most she will fetch, she is an old Ship & the sooner she is sold the better.

Thorndike was still in a pessimistic mood a month later, when he continued from where he had left off.

> Our La Plata Concern Looks Bad indeed, & has grown worse by the Improvidence of an Americans running away with a Cargo of Tallow belonging to a Spaniard, he has sent *me* out his Power [of attorney] & I have got possesn. of the Cargo, our last accounts from Tailor was on ye. 28th May the Sally was then nearly load'd & expected to sail in 10 to 30 days. There has been applica-

tion made to our govt. respectg. this unfortunate business, but they have not yet interfeared, & as it has been incouraged & licensed by *Colonial* officers who perhaps had no Authority from the *Mother Country* we cannot speak to the Spaniards in the same Language that we otherwise might, but I am sure that if the Amn. Gentleman should send an Agent to Madrid there is no person who they would prefer to yourself, & if you are serious I will set myself about putting the thing in Motion, and when you git there tip some of the Dons $\frac{1}{4}$ to $\frac{1}{2}$ of all savings from those adventures & they will understand the language perfectly.

The next paragraph suggests that Thorndike favored a conservative policy of overstating his losses so that in the final reckoning he might not be too disappointed.

Should we be so unfortunate as to loose the whole of this Concern, I believe we shall wind up better than we had a right to Expect considering the violence of the Squall in which we were cant aback.

An intervening letter is lost, but Dickason's reply reveals a much more relaxed and calm approach to the vicissitudes of business in a troubled world than do his American friend's deadly-serious communications.

London 2 March 1803

MY DR SIR

I was duly favor'd with your letter of 17 Octr & was grieved to learn that your Son was so unfortunate as to have a Complaint in his eyes. Young Gray who I presume is with you recd. great benefit from the Faculty here & I should hope would determine your sending your son this way without delay—& the whole of this Family will be happy to render him every friendly attention.

I observe you had just recd. a Letter from Taylor

which looks more favorable than anything you had
before recd. . . . I anticipate better luck than you do,
hoping to realize in these concerns first costs—but our
friend Sears will say I am too Sanguine. Should you
go to War with the Spaniards about the New Orleans
business, I must be out in America, to take my share of
dressing them—& get back my property which they have
held at La Plata.

Thorndike was still gloomy about the whole outlook on
June 1, 1803.

Our La Plata concerns looks badly we have no late
accounts from there, but if the Dons should git engaged
in War with G Britain thay may be induced to ease off
to enable them to set another trap, but if war should
actually take place we must have some adventure under
way from London with Russ ports &c.

The happy ending to the River Plate venture was finally
reported by Dickason, who was able to conclude with a rhap-
sodic soliloquy on a most prosaic theme!

London 16 August 1803
My dear Sir
I am favor'd with your much esteemed letters of 30
May and 1 June and most sincerely congratulate your
son on the recovery of his eye sight. I trust it will only
delay his visit to this country for a few years as I should
have real pleasure in seeing any part of your family here
indeed I have been hoping you would pay us a visit—
but now we have renewed the war in Europe [you] will
have enough to do in Beverly. You find our Là Plata Concerns have mended since you wrote. The sale of the Five
Brothers & Cargo and small sums received from Hambro.
on account Sally's Cargo will amount to something handsome. I hope that account will now be soon closed—

should you and our friend D [avid] S [ears] have
courage there will be no difficulty in shipping a Cargo
from France to La Plata with protecting papers against
British Cruizers & Perhaps as most of your country-
men may be averse to continuing that Trade it may
make it more favorable for those who do venture. The
ship China (formerly Peter Blights) has been offered at
public sale and no one bid upon £5000—1008 Tons live
oak and Cedar—oh! for some of your speculative spirit
and judgement—or some of mine such *as I had at Boston.*
What a glorious parcel of Tallow & Hides this ship
would carry.

THE UNHAPPY NEUTRAL

The blissful period of American maritime prosperity, when that
country was the happy neutral in a world torn by a titanic
struggle, did not last indefinitely. Far more serious than the
seizures in the Quasi-War with France in the late 1790's was the
steady grinding down of the American merchant marine caught
between Napoleon's Continental System and Britain's answering
Orders in Council.

First blood from Thorndike was drawn by the British ship-
of-war *Seahorse,* which captured the brig *Pembroke,* Captain
John Gardner, en route from Gallipoli to London and Copenhagen, on May 5, 1807. An eye-witness on the *Seahorse* reported,
"We chased her from one o'clock on the afternoon of May 4th
to half past four in the afternoon of May 5 when she was
brought to and boarded." The Court of Vice Admiralty at
Gibraltar declared the brig and her cargo of oil forfeit for
violation of the Order in Council of January 7, 1807, but certain
private ventures carried on board were released.

The next recorded capture was made by the other side. On
May 12, 1809, the schooner *Mary,* Captain Henry Larcom, was
seized by a Neapolitan gunboat, part of Joaquim Murat's navy,
two miles off Civita Vecchia, Tuscany. She was on her way from
Beverly to Sardinia laden with sugar, pepper and cotton to the

value of $18,067.32. The case was to be heard before the Council of State of Thirty-three, but it was postponed and postponed. Meanwhile the vessel leaked and the cargo of sugar was damaged. Finally the council decided in favor of Larcom, and the decision was sent to Paris for the emperor to endorse. But Napoleon reversed the council's decision and ordered the *Mary* and her cargo to be auctioned off for the state. From this edict there was no appeal. The *Mary* fetched only seven hundred and fifty dollars at auction, which Henry Larcom thought was fair enough, observing, "She is eaten quite through by the worms in some places." In reply to a protest by United States Consul Hammett in Naples, the Neapolitan Minister of Foreign Affairs had the effrontery to write that there would not be such confiscations when the United States proved more favorable to the French Empire!

Acting under the protection of the laws of the Continental System, designed to cut off commerce with Great Britain, Scandinavian privateersmen skulked about the entrance to the Baltic looking for shipping to seize. On April 30, 1809, such a privateer, of Danish registry, captured Thorndike's brig the *Suwarrow,* Captain William Leech, Jr., and carried her up the fjord into the Norwegian capital Christiania. The *Suwarrow* was laden with tobacco valued at twenty thousand dollars, intended for the Swedish port of Gothenburg. What particularly graveled Robert Rogers, supercargo of the vessel, who wrote the reports on the whole episode that were sent back to Thorndike, was that the owners and agents of the privateer boarded the captured *Suwarrow* in Christiania Harbor and "sat as inquisitors, interpreters & judges in their own cause." A legal trial was eventually promised by the local authorities, but it was long delayed. The Norwegian king gave orders to speed up the machinery of justice, but Rogers found that the royal orders were "no more regarded here, than the squallings of an impotent suckling." Young George Thorndike, Israel's second son, was aboard the brig at the time of her capture and he happened to have with him a copy of his "commencement Exercise," or baccalaureate thesis from Bowdoin College, on the subject of international trade. This document was produced by the privateers as legal evidence to justify the seizure of the vessel: George had spoken disparagingly of Napoleon!

The libeling of the *Suwarrow* took place in a Norwegian court of admiralty in November and December 1809. The captors first alleged that the brig was British, or that her cargo, at least, was British-owned. This line of argument was refuted to the satisfaction of the court, but this was scant comfort to the Americans, because the judgment went to the captors anyway, on their allegation that the vessel, at the time of her capture, had appealed to a British frigate for aid. Rogers characterized this accusation as "founded in *falsehood* & *supported* by the *blackest iniquity*." He reported further that the Norwegians complacently admitted that they felt no anxiety about condemning American shipping, because the United States would not go to war to help a few ships; if she did go to war, they continued, it would not hurt anybody, anyway. The whole experience was most galling for the young man from Beverly, Massachusetts. The final remark that made Rogers fulminate was the observation that the condemning of the brig *Suwarrow* was a punishment to Americans for repealing Jefferson's Embargo and an appropriate "antidote to their commercial mania." There was just enough truth in this last stricture on America's attempt to batten on the trade of war-ravaged Europe to give it a scorpion's sting. The *Suwarrow* was declared a total loss to the underwriters of the Essex Fire & Marine Insurance office.

It is clear throughout the accounts of these events that America and Americans were not looked upon with favor or respect by Europeans during the Napoleonic Wars.

Other casualties were the schooner *Dove,* the brig *Two Betseys* and the brig *Hector.* The *Hector* case formed the basis of a correspondence extending over a period of years between Thorndike and anyone with any political influence who would read his letters. The *Hector* was taken by a Russian frigate in the Gulf of Smyrna, carried to the Aegean island of Tenedos, and there condemned by a mock court held in the Russian admiral's cabin. After the cargo had been removed, the vessel herself was inadvertently destroyed when the Turks attacked the Russians. Evidence of Thorndike's shrewdness and deviousness appears in his explanation of the circumstances to Harrison Gray Otis. He wrote that the brig

> cleared out at Marseilles for Trieste although actually bound for Smyrna, the reason for this was to conceal the real destination of the vessel, lest other Americans should follow & thereby effect the market and from apprehension that, as the french & turks were, at that time, allies, the *English* might consider her as bound from one *enemy* port to *another*.

Thorndike wanted Otis, then a member of the Senate, to prod the government to do something about it. Business came first with Thorndike, but a personal note did intrude upon one of these hectoring letters. Israel Thorndike, Jr., had been married to Otis's daughter and had recently become widowed by her death. The elder Thorndike took a few lines to venture that it would help his son to keep the family together if they could board with Otis's mother.

The *Hector* case dragged along without incident for a number of years. On February 11, 1826, Thorndike wrote Edward Everett and begged him and Daniel Webster to use their influence with Clay and Adams to renew the demand for an indemnity from the Russian government for the seizure of the vessel and her cargo. He expressed a willingness to abide by the arbitration of the British representative in St. Petersburg, acting in concert with Middleton, the American minister. He hoped that the recent accession of Nicholas I, following the death of Alexander I, might presage a change in Russian policy. Thorndike's persistence and importunities finally paid off. John Quincy Adams notes in his *Memoirs* that on June 6, 1828, Mr. Clay came in with a dispatch from Russian Foreign Minister Count Nesselrode to Baron Krudener in Washington stating that Czar Nicholas had reviewed the long-standing claims concerning the *Hector* and another vessel in similar plight, the *Commerce,* and ordered a settlement agreeable to the claimants.

Trade with the Orient continued during these troubled and uncertain years, though at a slackened tempo. The ship *Alexander Hodgdon,* which we saw was purchased in 1802, remained in service on the old Sumatra run. The last we hear of her is when, in the summer of 1811, Thorndike wrote to the Philadelphia firm of Willing & Francis asking that an advertisement be sent to the newspapers announcing the auction on Thursday, August 8, 1811, at twelve noon, of the *Hodgdon*'s cargo of 750,000 pounds of pepper. The ship *Asia,* Captain Phineas Ellis, eight-tenths owned by Thorndike, was active in the India trade, and in January 1809 brought a return of $68,003.21 to her owners.

In the Mediterranean the schooner *Jeremiah,* Captain John Groves, and the brig *Hector,* before she was lost, were both reported doing business with Liquier, Bonhomme & Company in Marseilles in the summer of 1807. The schooner *Augusta,* Captain Joseph Stickney, sold West India produce to Lann Brothers of Bayonne on the Bay of Biscay in the late spring of 1809.

To sell West India goods abroad, Thorndike maintained his dealings with the Caribbean as long as he could. The ship *Hope,* Captain Pyam Lovett, (not to be confounded with the earlier schooner *Hope,* commanded by Captain Tarbox Moulton, in that same trade), did business with West Indian ports in 1807 and the winter of 1808–1809. This last venture caused the *Hope* to become the center of a heated controversy when she was accused of having violated Jefferson's Embargo by making an illegal voyage from the United States to Havana.

The commercial aspects of the Napoleonic Wars, comprising the Continental System, the British Orders in Council, the American Embargo and ultimately the War of 1812, spelled the beginning of the end of the purely maritime phase of the New England economy. There are no data with which to compare the "before" with the "after" conditions of Israel Thorndike's maritime business. One interesting figure concerning his prewar employment of seamen came out of the Massachusetts legislative hearing on British impressment. The largest employer of mariners listed was William Gray, who employed three hundred merchant seamen annually prior to 1812. Second to Gray was Thorndike, with a payroll of two hundred. The uncertainties of the later Napoleonic Era are reflected in Thorndike's affairs by a general decline in volume of trade. This decline shows up clearly in Thorndike's business papers, which then cease to be a reliable index of his shipping activities.

THE LEONARD INCIDENT

Andrew Thorndike, for whom the *Alexander Hodgdon* had been originally acquired, finally, after many attempts, resigned his position as supercargo in his uncle's employ and appears in the records dating from 1807 as a partner of Thorndike, Leonard & Company, Barcelona merchants. By September 5 of that year the firm was dissolved, following a violent disagreement between the partners Andrew Thorndike and John Leonard. There were charges and countercharges, and we cannot determine the merits of the case at this distance. A former employee of the concern, one William Goodwin, favored Andrew Thorndike and continued to act as Israel Thorndike's Barcelona agent.

Israel took sides in the dispute with some vigor, so that the episode is of some significance in indicating his feeling of family solidarity and his method of approach to this sort of personal problem. He wrote a letter to Timothy Pickering, at that time a United States Senator, and asked him, as an old friend, to approach the Foreign Service authorities and secure the appointment of his nephew's supporter Goodwin as an American consul in Catalonia. Then he added:

> At the same time that I should recommend Mr. Goodwin as a suitable man for this appointment I think it my duty to state that Mr. John Leonard, who is now Consul at Barcelona, has in his Consular capacity, conducted in a very improper manner; and has in two cases

of my own, refused to give his Consular certificates, to enable me to cancel my bonds at the Custom-House here, alledging for his justification, that he had a *dispute* with the *consignee;* and in consequence of his refusal to do his duty in this respect, my Agent was obliged to procure his certificates and all other Consular papers from the foreign resident Consuls. These facts can be substantiated by papers in my possession, and the certificates of the Danish Consul, now lodged in the Custom House at Salem.

I forbear to say any thing of Mr. Leonard's character as a factor, or a man of hon. & fair dealing; this can, if necessary, be shown by all the Masters & factors who have had any dealings with him.

If the President should think proper to remove Mr. Leonard as Consul for Barcelona, I think the place cannot be filled with a more suitable person than Mr. Goodwin.

Any interest you may take in promoting either one or the Other of the before mentioned objects will (in my opinion) be rendering valuable service to the community; or at least, the mercantile part of it.

This communication was sent from Beverly on January 8, 1810—more than two years after the row between Andrew Thorndike and John Leonard. Israel Thorndike was a man with a long memory and not always inclined to take the broadest view of a situation involving his own interest or prejudices.

POST-NAPOLEONIC VENTURES

For the period after the Vienna settlement there are only small pieces of evidence with which to attempt a reconstruction of Thorndike's maritime trade. In 1816 he owned the brigantine *Bramin,* 241 tons, in partnership with his former captain William Leech. From the habit of shipowners, particularly of the period in question, to name their vessels according to the trade for which they are intended, we may assume that the *Bramin* was an Indiaman and that Thorndike retained his interest in Far Eastern adventures after the close of the wars.

A smaller craft, registered in Thorndike's name in 1825, was the schooner *Boxer,* 73 tons, which suggests that in his preoccupation with the grand traffic with the Orient, he did not neglect the coastal ports and fisheries.

In 1803 his friend and sometime partner Thomas Dickason, Jr., had suggested that a profitable commerce might be developed with South America, and belatedly Thorndike heeded this advice. We find him sending goods, paper among other items, from Cadiz to Buenos Aires in 1818, taking advantage of the recent revolt of the South American colonies from Spain to furnish them with goods they had been accustomed to import from the mother country in Spanish bottoms. From the court action *Israel Thorndike vs. Samuel Hill, (Master Mariner),* which dragged on from 1822 to 1827, it is clear that he was engaged in 1817 in a trade between Chile and Canton. Copper was taken on at the South American country and carried to China in exchange for Oriental goods. The ship *Packet* was employed in this circuit.

The final key to Israel Thorndike's latter-day shipping activities is to be found in the inventory of his estate compiled following his death in 1832. Under the headings "Merchandize & Vessels" and "Schedule of Merchandize in New York, and Adventures at Sea" are enumerated his entire holdings at the cutoff date. These inventories show that while Thorndike devoted most of his later years to textile manufacturing, he did not for a moment let that interest preclude him from participating in his original line of business. At the time of his death his investments in mercantile ventures totaled almost $400,000. Bulk commodities owned in Boston amounted to $138,622.94. Bulk commodities in New York came to somewhat less, $114,781.20. Ships, ships' stores and odds and ends in Boston were estimated at $68,869.42, and "Adventures at Sea" added up to $73,100.87. Thorndike had been trading most heavily in tea, with silks a poor second, followed by wool and hemp, if the inventory of items on hand is an adequate measure of the relative values of the commodities dealt in. West Indian produce and Oriental goods other than tea had virtually disappeared from his warehouses by 1832, and he had so directed his executive gifts to the industrial development of New England that he owned but four vessels when he died, and one of those, the *Israel,* only through repossession following Captain Israel Stone's failure to make good his purchase of 1826.

The inventory of Thorndike's estate gives a suggestion as to what manner of place it was in which the man carried on his business and planned his voyages. His counting house in later years was at 53 Central Wharf, Boston, to which he had moved from the old premises at 45 India Wharf after 1825. It was an unpretentious establishment, in keeping with the English and New England feeling against ostentation in business rooms, which might give the visitor too clear an insight into the prosperity of the firm or, on the other hand, detract from the concern's reputation for conservative solidity. The furniture—seventy-five dollars' worth, according to the inventory—was sparse and undoubtedly worn. There was doubtless a desk for Thorndike himself, and perhaps there were some stand-up desks and high stools for the few clerks who copied letters and wrote figures into ledgers under the eyes of a succession of confidential chief clerks, whom we know to have included Dwight Boyden, in the Beverly period, and after him, in Boston, Augustus Lovett, Sr., and John Gibson. There was some disorder, too, if not in the counting room itself, at least in the loft and cellar, where the "Lot of old muskets, casks & sundries" of the inventory were stored. The warehouse adjoined, and what wonderful smells must have permeated the place from the bags of coffee and pepper, the bales of hemp and the Chinese chests which were piled high within!

THREE

Life in Beverly

THE COUNTRY SQUIRE

The year 1792 found Israel Thorndike admitting to a greater degree of prosperity than heretofore by the act of purchasing a fine house and acquiring piecemeal a considerable tract of land adjoining. A series of six entries in the deed records of Essex County for December 27, 1792, shows that during the year Thorndike had made one major purchase and a number of lesser ones. For the sum of fourteen hundred pounds he bought from Lydia Cabot, widow of the merchant Andrew Cabot, the brick dwelling house which was to be spoken of and pointed out for years afterwards as his "Beverly seat." For lesser amounts he picked up a "piece of tillage" on one side of him, twenty-one and three-quarter acres of pasture land on another side and other parcels until he had built up a large property comprising much of that part of the modern town of Beverly lying between the business district and the shore.

In the late eighteenth century this whole area was a thinly populated stretch of farm and woodland cut by streams busily turning mill wheels. Mercantile activity was concentrated at the southern tip of the town opposite Salem and there a dozen or so wharves jutted out from Water Street. Even at this late date codfish were spread out in the sun to cure in the very heart of the town and contemporary travelers tell of the unpleasant smell.

Lucy Larcom recalled the prosperous scene of Thorndike's Beverly estate in her book of memoirs *A New England Girlhood,* written almost a century later. She remembered nostalgically

> ... the finest house in town, a three-story edifice of brick, painted white, the "Colonel's" residence. There was a spacious garden behind it, from which we caught glimpses and perfumes of unknown flowers. Over its high walls hung boughs of splendid great yellow sweet apples, which, when they fell on the outside, we children considered our perquisites. When I first read about the apples of the Hesperides, my idea of them was that they were like the Colonel's "pumpkin-sweetings."
>
> Beyond the garden were wide green fields which reached eastward down to the beach. It was one of those large old estates which used to give to the very heart of our New England coast-towns a delightful breeziness and roominess.
>
> A coach-and-pair was one of the appurtenances of this estate, with a coachman on the box; and when he took the family out for an airing we small children thought it was a sort of Cinderella-spectacle, prepared expressly for us.

It was doubtless for the cultivation of these rolling acres that one Andrew Cheaver rendered his bill on November 3, 1803, for "plowing and halling dung."

An article in the *Beverly Citizen* of April 3, 1886, gives a more detailed description of the house and grounds in their prime.

> It was built of brick. The walls in the two lower stories were eighteen inches thick, and the upper or third story walls were twelve inches thick, the finish of the inside of the house being very elaborate, having been done in

Israel Thorndike's house in Beverly

(*From a watercolor in the Beverly Historical Society*)

the old English Battalangly style, with heavy, wide, thick architraves, with windows and door-heads, solid wainscoting with heavy base and impost mouldings, very elaborate mantels, mahogany tops, with solid paneling above and returned on the chimney breast at the sides. Windows finished with box-paneled shutters, the frieze of the window and door heads being finished with swelled front. All the inside and outside panel doors were made with double panels and put together with double tenons and mortises, block cornices in all the rooms of the two lower stories.

A magnificent hall way and stair case, finished in Battalangly's best style of art, with square landings, heavy moulded stair-rail, moulded and twisted balusters placed alternately, each tread of stairs being paneled underneath. No pains were spared in the finish of the china closet and store-room with all the known conveniences of that time. The outside of the mansion was finished in exceedingly good taste and style. The roof was four-sided, or hip, with a handsome pitch, leaving a flat or deck at the top, enclosed with a heavy balustrade composed of a heavy base and impost, with turned heavy four-inch balusters. The coving of the house with its cornice and blocked dented bed-mould was in good taste and was highly ornamental.

The house had two fronts, one on the main street, and the other at the south, and known as the garden front, as it opened into the garden and lawn. Both entrances were provided with porticoes with pediment front of the Roman Ionic style of architecture, and were of great beauty and symmetry. In front of the house was a pale fence, the posts being ornamented with pilasters and carved modern Ionic capitals. This fence was a segment of a circle directly in front of the house, the remainder of the fence being in a straight line. The whole garden was surrounded by white-pine trees which had grown, most of them, to the height of from thirty

to forty feet. The garden was well stocked with fruit
trees, laid out with gravel walks, lined with box ever-
green and well supplied with choice flowers and shrub-
bery of various kinds, many being of foreign extraction.

It is difficult to reconcile these descriptions of a gracious,
formal house with the building's present mutilated appearance
as the boxlike, down-at-the-heel Beverly Town Hall. Thorndike's
heirs sold out in 1841 for six thousand five hundred dollars.

The architect "Battalangly" will, of course, be identified at
once as Batty Langley (1696–1751), whose bold Italianate designs
of ornamental building details exerted enormous influence in
the Georgian Era through the medium of the builder's guide
or copybook. He was the author of *The City and Country
Builder's and Workman's Treasury of Designs: or the Art of
Drawing and Working the Ornamental Parts of Architecture*
(1750), and *The Builder's Jewel: or the Youth's Instructor and
Workman's Remembrancer* (1754).

Other particulars about Thorndike's handsome residence
come from various sources. It is recalled that when arrangements
were being made for converting the place into a public building
in 1841, there was a fight in the committee over whether or not
to retain the scenic wallpaper on the library walls. The bald
inventory of the house's contents under the heading "Furniture
in Mansion House at Beverly" in the *Inventory and Appraise-
ment of the Estate of the Hon. Israel Thorndike late of the City
of Boston,* dated July 30, 1832, tells us little enough. The
contents of the "Front Parlour" were catalogued as "Carpet, sofa,
4 engravings, Rocking chair, centre table, Piano, work-table,
9 chairs, &c . . . $243.00."

It was in these opulent surroundings that Israel Thorndike,
whose inheritance had come to one pound four shillings, set
up as a country squire and entertained the great and near-great
of his day. Here the celebration of Independence Day at Beverly
on July 4, 1807, reached its climax at half past nine, when the
Light Infantry Company paraded "in front of Hon. Israel
Thorndike's mansion" and "received the present of a standard,"

according to the standard history of the town. Here Robert Rantoul recalled in his "Reminiscences" that, ". . . in 1809, Mr. Thorndike opened his house for the public reception of Governor Christopher Gore, who made a tour from Boston to Maine with much parade. I was introduced to Governor Gore in Mr. Thorndike's house, in company with the other officers of the Militia in military dress with swords." And here, as will be seen, President Monroe was sumptuously received in August 1817, at the beginning of the Era of Good Feelings.

There are indications that Israel Thorndike tended to overlook his modest origins and to take himself very seriously in later life, after he had become prosperous. It is clear that his criterion of social status was strictly in line with the Boston tradition. Money counted most. This is brought out in a letter from his captain, Samuel Hill, to John P. Cushing in Canton, dated March 8, 1823. Speaking of a disagreeable encounter with his employer, Hill wrote that Thorndike had said "that he did not intend to be very hard with me, & fain would persuade me to believe that he never doubted my Integrity, only that he believed I was too Independent for a man of my class."

Not all of Thorndike's old neighbors were overawed by his rise to fortune. There was the case of one forthright Beverly citizen who wrote on May 18, 1807, beginning, "Billy Porter Presents his Compliments to Col. Israel Thorndike." Billy Porter then immediately got to the point—would the colonel give him some cabbage plants, he wanted to know!

HOMELY MATTERS

Small glimpses of Israel Thorndike's private life emerge from scraps of bills and memoranda that got mixed in with his business papers and so are preserved in part in the *Israel Thorndike Papers.*

A year after the death of his first wife, Mercy Trask Thorndike, he married Anna Dodge of Salem, on October 31, 1784. This was a most prolific union, and a number of household bills remain relating to the upbringing and schooling of this large family, and to the running of the extensive establishment already described.

On July 6 and 7, 1792, the son of one David Forni worked on the Thorndike farm at wages of four shillings a day.

Young Israel Thorndike, Jr., was stricken ill in the summer of 1795. The physician, William Wilkins, rendered a bill for sixteen visits and medicines which totalled one pound seventeen shillings sixpence. In these early years of the republic American dollars and British pounds were both used freely in business transactions. Israel, Jr., would have been something under ten years old at this time. He was born on December 2, 1785. This lad was sent off to Billerica, Massachusetts, in the fall, after his illness, to attend the academy of Ebenezer Pemberton. This was not a boarding school, so he took lodgings in the town, at the home of Joshua Abbot, who noted on his bill to the father for board and nursing while ill that the boy "behaved very well." There are a number of school bills among the Thorndike papers, indicating Israel's determination that his children should receive the education which he had been denied.

Purchases of both food and clothing for the household were made by Mrs. Anna Dodge Thorndike at the general store kept by Mary Campbell. Wages for domestic service are shown by various bills, including one from Elizabeth Down for $27.45 for forty-seven weeks' service at three shillings sixpence monthly. This gives us a conversion ratio for dollars and shillings of slightly less than six shillings to the dollar.

Israel, Jr., continued to go to school in Billerica until 1799. Ebenezer Pemberton charged tuition at the rate of £2/6/10, or $7.80 (he submitted figures in both currencies on his statements), per semester. The following year the boy went up to Haverhill to be taught by the Reverend Abiel Abbott. By July 1800, George Thorndike, now eleven, named after an elder brother who had died in infancy, joined young Israel at Abiel Abbott's. In the next year both lads were sent up to Phillips Exeter Academy, where one of them promptly dislocated his arm, as noted in a doctor's bill of May 1801. The brothers boarded at Exeter with Deacon Brooks. The academy itself billed their father, for the term ending October 1801, one hundred and twenty dollars for the two. In addition to board bills and term bills, a recurring expense was shoe leather. Young Israel and George frequently had to buy new shoes or have the old ones repaired. Clothes and quill pens were purchased by the young scholars at Exeter Village. Hats came from Albert Gray's emporium, nearer home.

While the older boys were away at school, Charles and Edward received instruction in Beverly from Miss Eliza Champney, daughter of the minister. An unexplained educational expense on Miss Champney's bills is the charge for tuition for children apparently not related to the Thorndike family, and possibly belonging to members of the domestic staff, to judge by their surnames. Polly Barrett, Rebekah Cheaver, Hannah Standley and Nancy Down all had their schooling paid for by the Thorndikes. Eliza Champney accepted her pupils at a very tender age. Her bill of November 3, 1803, lists Master Oliver, who could have been only three and a half at the time, since he was born on March 4, 1800.

To have a pair of boy's pantaloons made to order in March 1802 by John P. Taylor, whose name designated his occupation, cost four shillings sixpence. In 1802 the Thorndike household purchased peppermint at the rate of a bottle every fortnight. This condiment, or medicament, was purveyed by Mrs. Eliza Ives.

There was sickness in the house late in the summer of 1802, and Dr. Isaac Rand attended at a charge of four dollars for three visits.

Schooling continued to be an important item in the family budget. School supplies for the period June 24 to July 22, 1802, came to $1.52½ at John Sawyer's shop. Israel, Jr., was brought up by his father to treat even the most modest sums in a businesslike manner. He was required to submit financial statements at intervals, listing paid bills in the left-hand column, against the opposing entries, headed "Cash Received from My Father." His statement of August, 1802 from Exeter totaled $29.09 and included the item of $3.50 for "going to the Beach."

By 1802, George Thorndike had left Exeter and gone down

to Brunswick in the District of Maine to attend Bowdoin College. During his first year he boarded with the Reverend William F. Rowland, who charged him $2.50 a week. The next year he boarded with Robert D. Dunning, whose bill, rendered in February 1803, was $27.05 for "board and firewood." Students at Bowdoin at the beginning of the century lived in the college dormitories but took their meals in town. George Thorndike's bill from the President and Trustees of Bowdoin College for "Term No. 1," 1803, was for seven dollars, of which $5.33 was for tuition and $1.67 for room rent. Happily for the elder Thorndike's peace of mind and pocketbook, there were blanks opposite the printed items "To damages done to his chamber," "To average of damages done to college buildings" and "To fines for breach of college laws." George seems to have done himself pretty well down at Brunswick. His purchases included "Olive velvet" and "Brown Holland silk." Others in the family were splurging a bit on dress in that same year of 1803. A bill from Callendar & Jenkins, 4 State Street, Boston, dated January 13 (and paid the following August 26) totaled $129.27 and cited an infantry uniform, at $27, and a pair of corded-velvet pantaloons, both specified as for one of the Thorndike sons. George favored the store of John Swartkin in Brunswick for his purchases of candles, soap and the Malaga wine which was such an appropriate accompaniment to his brave attire. He, too, was required to keep accounts, and his statement for three college terms in 1803 lists expenditures in the amount of $228.66. The triumphant climax of George Thorndike's career at Bowdoin College is noted in Parson Bentley's diary, in the entry for August 29, 1806. He wrote: "Great preparations in this quarter for a visit to Brunswick to be present at the first Commencement in Maine. A Son of Col. Thorndike in Beverly is among the Graduates."

Household expenses for the latter part of 1802 included the purchase of 13½ yards of diaper for $6.75, and William Blythe's bill for $93.18 for painting the carriage and the chaise and painting the floor of the house a green color. Mrs. Cross, the seamstress, worked for the family that fall and charged Mrs. Thorndike nine shillings for "1 pair galises for George," three shillings for "making gown for yourself," six shillings sixpence for a coat for Andrew and nine shillings for cutting clothes for Charles and Edward.

Israel Thorndike had his barbering done in Beverly by William Backford, who sent his bills quarterly. "Shaving and Dressing" and "cutting 5 childrens hare" for the quarter ended January 1, 1803, amounted to $4.50, and for the next three-month period these items came to $5.00. A bill later in the year contained a charge for "One pound of hare Powder," an appropriate purchase for a Federalist, given that party's adherence to aristocratic traditions of coiffure and dress.

Robert Rantoul, the apothecary, sold the family their medicines and sundries, which included saltpeter, camphor and tincture of rhubarb. Thorndike patronized William Norton's livery stable, though possessing horses and carriages of his own. Items appearing on Norton's bill of February 26, 1803, are "Horse and Slaigh," "Shaise to Exeter" and "Damagin the harnis"—all of which totaled $5.50.

Young Andrew Thorndike, born August 28, 1790, and named for his paternal grandfather, had a bad winter in 1802–03 and was under the care of Dr. John D. Treadwell of Salem (who submitted a bill for $12.50 on April 19, 1803). He was well enough to go to Exeter later in 1803, however, and there he boarded with Simeon Brown. The following year he first attended Phillips Andover Academy and later was taught by Ebenezer Pemberton of Billerica. This rapid succession of schools leads to the suspicion that Andrew might have been something of a problem to his teachers. There was also some trouble over his board bill at Samuel Whiting's in Billerica in the summer of 1805. Andrew said he had lost the money his father had given him to pay his landlord.

Meanwhile the younger children were coming along and reaching the age to be sent away to school. Edward was at school in Salem in 1802, while Charles and Augustus were at

Lynn. The next year all three boys boarded with Joseph Dana while attending Lynn Academy. The year 1806 found Edward and Charles emulating their dashing older brother George in dressing like the sons of a prosperous merchant. Each bought a tall silk hat at Benjamin Loring's shop at twelve shillings apiece. They shared one bottle of shoe blacking at three shillings. They were still little boys, and it was only a few months before that Charles had received a bill for "Repairing Battledors."

Edward Thorndike did not stay at Exeter. In September 1807 he was in school at Hampton Falls, where he remained during the following year, though his health was not good, as is shown by a memorandum of "15 days abs." and Dr. Ebenezer Lawrence's bill for five visits. Andrew joined his brother at Hampton Falls— here is still another change of schools—and the two were there together in the spring of 1808.

There was a good deal of sickness in the Thorndike family. Israel had been much concerned about the health of his eldest son, Israel, Jr., in the fall of 1803 and wrote to the Reverend Joseph McKeen of Brunswick, with whom George had boarded the previous spring, to ask if he would take the young man with him on a contemplated trip to South Carolina and Savannah, Georgia, and keep him under his "Care & patronage."

Israel was also interested in providing his family with more of the amenities of civilized living than just formal schooling. Presumably this was his intent when he bought $79.65 worth of books at auction on December 29, 1802. In the lot were thirteen volumes of David Hume's *History of England;* Robinson's treatises on India, America and Scotland; assorted works by Terence, Sallust and Virgil, and the collected writings of Thomas Otway, redoubtable author of *The Orphan, or The Unhappy Marriage.* Several of the children took music lessons. One Amos Sawyer repaired a flute for Israel in the summer of 1803. (He also repaired an umbrella and sold the family three dozen spoons for two dollars a dozen; his total bill was for $7.42) Andrew bought an "instrumental Assistant" in 1805 and there were purchases of violin strings in both 1805 and 1806.

The business of running a large house kept right on even though some members of the family were away at school. Anna Thorndike paid five shillings twopence a yard for linen in September 1805. Homely items such as a stoneware dish, a coffee-pot and a cheese taster appear on the household bills along with hats, one a "Leghorne," later that fall. The following April the dressmaker Emma Hammond came to the house. She moved right in and remained for five strenuous days of letting out hems and outfitting the family with new clothes. Garments for the domestic staff were also turned out by this energetic seamstress. Doubtless she outfitted the ladies of the household with those newfangled bifurcated garments, underdrawers, which Alice Morse Earle tells us in her *Two Centuries of Costume in America* had come into the wardrobe at the turn of the century with the sheer India dress materials. Emma Hammond's charges for the five-day period were $15.18.

The servants were not paid very often at the Thorndikes'. Sally Carrol asked for $154.57 for seventy-seven weeks and two days—wages due April 30, 1807, at two dollars a week. Ten years before, in the good old days when domestics received only sixty cents weekly, Elizabeth Down had been paid at the end of forty-seven weeks.

FOUR

Speculation

WESTERN LANDS

A single letter in the great welter of correspondence and business memoranda that makes up the *Israel Thorndike Papers* opens up the whole matter of Thorndike's flyer in Western lands. This is the last item in the 1801 file, the copy of a communication to Ephraim Root dated Beverly, September 15, 1801. The letter acknowledges the receipt of various drafts totaling six thousand dollars "which shall be Indorsed (when Rec'd in Cash) on your & Mr. Wyles Bond, being on acct. of Interest & principle of the same." The origin of the bond is revealed in the next paragraph.

> I have not seen Mr. Prescott since I Rec'd your letter but I think he will prefer keeping his Share of the Western Reserve lands rather than Selling them on the terms you mention as does your Friend & Humble
> Servant
> I. T.

This is the first clue to Thorndike's involvement in the historic Ohio real-estate venture, but with this to start from, the whole story unfolds, revealing another area of operations, one which interested Israel Thorndike throughout almost half his lifetime.

Ohio was a familiar name to Beverly citizens. They could well remember the departure of Dr. Cutter's little band of pioneers bound for that western wilderness. Perhaps it was the recollection of this Beverly connection with Ohio that stimulated Thorndike's interest.

The name of Israel Thorndike does not appear on the roster of purchasers of the Western Reserve of Connecticut, the group loosely organized into the Connecticut Land Company. His role was that of a silent partner, together with William Prescott, Jr., to John Wyles of Hartford, who was a formally recorded proprietor.

The Connecticut Land Company came into being in the fall of 1795 in Hartford as the result of the decision of the Connecticut legislature to get rid of the Western land remaining in that state's titular possession after the newly united states agreed in 1786 to give up their several ambitious claims to vast tracts extending across the continent. A committee of eight was instructed to sell an estimated three million acres of what is now Ohio land for a minimum of one million dollars, with the stipulation that they were to be disposed of as a bloc and not piecemeal. A syndicate of thirty-five individuals was formed, and it agreed on September 2, 1795, to raise $1,200,000 to buy the Western Reserve of Connecticut. Cash was not required at the outset, but the Committee of Eight gave bonds to the state treasurer in Hartford in return for a mortgage on the land. The individual purchasers went through a similar transaction, so we find Thorndike and Prescott putting up money in 1801 to cover their bond taken out jointly in the name of John Wyles.

The new territory was surveyed and divided into ranges—strips of land five miles wide running north and south and numbered from east to west, beginning at the Pennsylvania line. The ranges were then cut up into townships five miles square, numbered from south to north, starting at the forty-first parallel. When this elaborate gridiron had been laid out, the land was distributed by lot. A conscientious effort was made in the course

of the drawing to divide the good and the poor land on an
equitable basis among the proprietors, very much as was done
in the apportionment of strips in the two- and three-field systems
of mediaeval Europe. The result in both cases was that the
various parcels of a given landholder might be widely scattered.

The principal tract allocated to the partnership of Wyles,
Thorndike and Prescott was Township 2, Range 9, a parcel of
14,392 acres in Portage County. A large part of this allotment
was swamp, so the Equalizing Committee of the Connecticut
Land Company added a block of 7,380 acres in Township 7,
Range 8, near the town of Burton in Geauga County. Title to
these parcels was conveyed by the three trustees of the land
company on October 9, 1798. On April 25, 1807, the partners
received title to another substantial block of land, comprising
one half of Township 1 and part of Township 2, Range 15, near
Seville in Medina County. At the same time they were assigned
a city lot, No. 77, on Superior Street in Cleveland.

John Wyles attended to the management of these vast holdings
through his agent on the ground, Turhand Kirtland. A few
letters from Wyles in East Hartford to Kirtland in Poland, Trum-
bull County, Ohio, are preserved in the library of the Western
Reserve Historical Society, Cleveland, and these give some indication of the thinking of the speculators with regard to the
disposition of their land. Wyles wrote to Kirtland on September
21, 1807, that he and Israel Thorndike had agreed to sell Township 2, Range 9; would Kirtland please get the best parts of this
tract surveyed for subdivision. The following month he asked
Kirtland to collect money from those who still owed on their
bonds and to pay the taxes. He wanted to see the field book of
the survey. Enclosed was a power of attorney from the three partners authorizing Kirtland to sell the land in their interest.
Wyles instructed his agent to sell the first parcels for as little
as two dollars an acre to encourage settlement, but to raise the
price as the population increased. On November 30 he cautioned
Kirtland to sell good and bad land together as often as possible
so that the partners would not find themselves stuck with a lot
of worthless property. He also gave orders that mineral and

quarry lands were not to be sold for the present and urged, "Reserve some good lots for a future day."

There is a three-year gap in the correspondence, from the fall of 1807 to the fall of 1810. Wyles's letter to Kirtland of September 21, 1810, the next item in the collection, lacks something of the optimism presumably characteristic of land speculators. Wyles hoped there would soon be a "long list of sails of land" and deplored the fifteen hundred acres of water and "swamps that are good for nothing nor never will be." He apparently forgot that some compensation had already been made for these inferior acres. Actually, he underestimated the potentialities of the Portage County property, and so did the Equalizing Committee, or that body might not have been so generous. The swamps, when drained, turned out to be extremely rich farming country, though of course the partners did not live to see this.

The correspondence with Kirtland was continued by John Wyles, Jr., who inherited his father's interest in the Western Reserve upon the latter's death. Writing during the War of 1812, he observed to the agent: "A dreary time indeed for Land Speculators, but we are at this time [January 22, 1814] a little cheer'd up with a very distant prospect of Peace. Should it take place I am in hopes that you will be able to extend the Sales of Land hereafter." In July 1814 he wrote that one Samuel Fowler had petitioned for a division of lands held undivided in common, and that he and Thorndike and Prescott also favored a partition. He mentioned incidentally that he had recently removed to Brimfield, Massachusetts, a fact not without significance in Portage County, as will be seen.

In the spring of 1815, Israel Thorndike resolved to take a more active part in promoting his interest in the Western land. He gave half of his total holdings to his nephew Henry Thorndike, a lawyer residing in FitzWilliam, New Hampshire. Henry was to go out to Ohio with his family, settle in the Western Reserve, and act for his uncle in disposing of the property. The conveyance is on file at the Cuyahoga County Courthouse in Cleveland. It is dated Boston, May 12, 1815, and gives a full and detailed description of all land held jointly by Thorndike,

Prescott and the late Wyles (misspelled "Willis") on the given date. One half of Israel Thorndike's share was estimated to total 4,185 acres, leaving a like amount of land still in his possession after Henry had received the deed and power of attorney.

The *History of Portage County, Ohio* (1885) says that Israel Thorndike and John Wyles, Jr., actually came out to Ohio in 1816 to supervise the partition of their joint holdings. "They found . . . Town 2, Range 9, an unbroken wilderness, with nothing but wild beasts as its inhabitants, and they had no difficulty in making the division. Thorndike chose the north and Wyles the south half." This account goes on to state that Henry Thorndike arrived with his wife and children in November 1816, and that with them came his unmarried brother Israel A. Thorndike. Not long afterwards the settlers were joined by their cousin Edward Thorndike, Israel's sixth child by his second marriage. The *History* notes that Israel A. and Edward Thorndike started a nail factory west of the Center; it failed, however, and their saw mill also had to be abandoned.

The township was first called Swamptown, for obvious reasons, and later Beartown, for reasons quite as readily apparent. This latter name gave way to Greenbriar, which in turn yielded to Wylestown. When the meeting was called in 1818 to organize the town government at the Center—a meeting at which Henry Thorndike was elected a trustee and his brother the town treasurer—a proposal from Israel Thorndike, Sr., back in Boston, was read and submitted to the pioneer electorate. The *History* informs us that "Thorndike offered to give a plat of ground for a public square at the Center, if they would call it Thorndike, which was agreed to and it was so named officially. . . ." One looks in vain, however, for the town or village of Thorndike on modern maps of Portage County, Ohio. The *History* has an interesting explanation for this. It concludes the passage just quoted: ". . . but the old 'Injun Giver' backed out of the contract and would not make a deed for the ground, so the citizens petitioned and had the name changed to Brimfield, in honor of John Wyles, Jr., [who] resided in the town of Brimfield, Hampden Co., Mass." The entry in Jenkins Warren's

The Ohio Gazetteer and Traveler's Guide, published in 1837, reads: "Brimfield (Thorndike until 1830)."

Israel Thorndike's will, dated March 25, 1830, provided in paragraph fifteen that all lands and buildings belonging to him in Thorndike, Ohio, and Stow, Summit County, Ohio, were to become the property of the two sons of his own son Edward, who had predeceased him.

MAINE LANDS

Soon after he began his unsuccessful venture in Western Reserve lands Israel Thorndike became involved in similar speculations nearer home. This time the property was in the District of Maine, and since the affair started out as a simple mortgage loan, Thorndike probably did not realize at the outset that he was going to be a landed proprietor in that area.

As far back as 1791, General Henry Knox, the hearty, blustering, Gargantuan hero of the Revolutionary War, began pouring money into Maine real estate. In the summer of 1796 he took up residence at Montpelier, the magnificent house he had built at Thomaston on lands inherited by his wife from her maternal grandfather, Samuel Waldo. Still plunging recklessly, Knox embarked simultaneously upon a number of costly business enterprises and eventually became hopelessly involved. On April 3, 1799, Knox borrowed eight thousand dollars from Israel Thorndike, pledging land in Maine as security and further shoring up his sagging credit by signing penalty bonds for double the amount of the loan. He prevailed upon his old comrades-in-arms Henry Jackson and Benjamin Lincoln to stand as sureties for his bonds, and caused them serious financial embarrassment in consequence.

Knox was quite unable to meet interest payments and hypothecated more of his property to Thorndike. Meanwhile Thorndike invited William Prescott, Jr., of Salem, his associate in the Ohio deals, to join him in loans to Knox. Poor Knox seems to have had no business sense and he was no more able to repay principal than he had been able to pay interest. When the note held jointly by Thorndike and Prescott fell due in 1805, Thorndike drove from Beverly down to Maine to look the situation over for himself. He was apparently convinced that a fortune could be made in Maine real estate. Upon his return he wrote Knox a most disingenuous letter.

Beverly, 27th July 1805

My dear Sir,

I returned home from my journey the evg before last, & have very much to regret that the want of time & other circumstances (the badness of the horses which I hired at Portland being the chief) prevented my accepting your polite & friendly invitation to make you a visit at your seat in Thos. Town. I hope however to have that pleasure at some future day.

The note which fell due a few days since on which some conversation took place at Saco (youl. please to recollect) is not paid, circumstanced as I am as to the want of money, & having said to Mr. Prescott that he might depend on punctuality it would rearly give me great pleasure to have you order your agent in Boston to discharge it or take some other effectual measures to do it without further loss of time, & I hope youl. find it convenient to do it within thirty days.

Haveing had some conversation with you respecting ownership of an Island & Township *near* it, I will thank you to describe to me the situation, settlement, growth of wood, rivers & *lowest price*, & if you have any other *good* lands favourable for Settlement which you are disposed to sell on *favourable terms*, I will purchase of you to the amt. of $20,000 & I will pay you the Cash down & you may with confidence name to me your *lowest* price & if I do not acceed to your proposals, I pledge myself not to make any use of the information in any way to your disadvantage, please to send me an answer as soon as convenient.

Mrs. Thorndike and myself intreat our respects to
Mrs. Knox & your family, & I am with Sincere Regard,
your friend &

> Humble servant
> ISRAEL THORNDIKE

HON. GENL. KNOX

The inconsistency of Thorndike's poor mouth over his
alleged "want of money" and his offer to buy Maine land to
the value of twenty thousand dollars in cash could hardly have
escaped the rotund general. But any feelings of exasperation
he might have had on this score could only have been alleviated
by the prospect of laying his hands on some real money.

Thorndike and Prescott took title to 47,651 acres in Hancock
County on March 4, 1806, for a consideration of $15,200. Pre-
sumably funds already advanced as loans to Knox figured
in the purchase.

In June of the same year Thorndike wrote to his sometime
partner in maritime ventures, David Sears, and invited him to
come into the Maine land picture on any terms he desired. Heretofore Thorndike and Prescott had been playing for small
change. Now, with Sears as a backer, they bought vast tracts
of wilderness in eastern Maine which even to this day are
undeveloped. Within a month of broaching the matter to
Sears, Thorndike created a new partnership in which he and
Sears participated with seven-sixteenths of an interest each and
Prescott tagged along cautiously with two sixteenths. In a
statement of purchase dated July 25, 1806, the total investment
of the partners on that date, exclusive of prior acquisitions by
any of the participants, was determined to be $157,517. This
meant, according to the agreed formula, that Thorndike and
Sears were in for $68,913.69 apiece and Prescott had contributed
$19,689.62. The transaction was not on a cash basis. Each partner
gave Knox a series of five promissory notes payable in four
months, one year, sixteen months, two years and three years,
respectively.

A total of 117,700 acres of land was involved, from which ten thousand acres were subtracted as having already been sold to individual settlers by Henry Knox. The individual parcels before adjustment were in six blocks, as follows:

  9,000 acres in Lincolnsville, Northport and Camden
50,000 acres in tract "held in trust for Mrs. Swan"
15,000 acres in Prospect
25,000 acres in Bonaparte and Greene
16,000 acres in the Swan tract
  2,700 acres "round Belfast."

The net holdings of the partnership as of July 25, 1806, totaled 107,700 acres, most of which were purchased at the rate of $1.71 per acre. The members of Thorndike's trio were still not content with the empire they had acquired, and the records of deeds at Ellsworth, county seat of Hancock County, show that they continued to augment their enormous property with a series of small purchases during the following several months.

Then they began to sell.

Sales went briskly enough and a great number of individual transactions is recorded. Unfortunately for the entrepreneurs, however, the separate deals were on a very small scale, and as persons interested in pioneering a wilderness are characteristically short of capital, most of the sales were in mortgages rather than cash.

By 1816, Israel Thorndike was ready to get out from under the entire Maine land speculation. On January 4, 1816, he turned over virtually all of his Maine holdings to his eldest son, Israel, Jr., who appears thereafter as a frequent grantor of lands in the Hancock County deed records. The actual language of the document transferring ownership helps to clarify the whole situation for us.

I, Israel Thorndike . . . for and in consideration of my natural love and affection for my Son Israel Thorndike Junior of . . . Boston merchant, and for and in consideration of the sum of one thousand dollars by the said Israel Junior to me paid, . . . have . . . sold to said Israel Junior, all my seven undivided sixteenth parts of all the Lands and Tenements owned and held by me in common & undivided with David Sears & William Prescott, Esquires, situate in the Counties of Hancock and Lincoln & within the Waldo Patent, also the large dwelling House lately built by said David, William & myself and the Farm adjoining situate in the Plantation of Jackson in said County of Hancock and all the farming utensils and stock of every kind upon said Farm . . . and all my share . . . in a tract of land . . . at a place called Muscongus in the Eastern part of the Commonwealth . . . said tract of land comprising the town of Frankfort in said County of Hancock, and also a small tract without the bounds of said township.

The deed concludes with a summary and exception:

. . . meaning hereby to convey to said Israel Thorndike Junior all the lands and tenements in the District of Maine of which I am seized or entitled to be seized in fee or in mortgage, except such as I hold as security for debts arising from my mercantile concerns, and all my Stock of Cattle and Sheep of every kind in said District.

Again Thorndike is revealed as fundamentally interested in trade, seaborne trade, but with roots still in the soil.

Three months after conveying the bulk of his Maine property to his eldest son he gave further evidence of his characteristic feeling of family solidarity. On March 12, 1816, he wrote to Timothy Pickering in Washington in an attempt to use political pressure to improve the value of young Israel's real estate in the town of Frankfort, Hancock County.

I am inform'd that the inhabitants of Frankfort & some others on the Penobscot have recently petition'd Congress to establish a Port of Entry at that place.

I am well acquainted with the local situation of Frankfort & I am decidedly of the opinion that the request of the Petitioners is not unreasonable, but I cannot better describe the necessity & the superior advantages that Frankfort enjoys over any other place than by refering you to the enclosed letter which I have received from a friend of mine who is an inhabitant of Frankfort, & shall be willing to vouch for the correctness of his statement. I would however add one more fact against Buckstown being made a Port of entry, that it is on the coast side of the Penobscot, & so is Castine where the Custom House now is & I believe that it joins Castine, & I am Certain that the public interest & convenience would be more promoted by making Frankfort a Port of Entry than it would be my making Buckstown a Port of entry.

The petition and Thorndike's expression of his deep concern for the public weal did not bring a custom house to Frankfort, but old Israel worked on the principle that there was no harm in trying.

FIVE

Politics

THE FEDERALIST PARTY

At the Beverly Town Meeting of March 12, 1781, the assembled citizenry elected Israel Thorndike to the office of constable with its function of tax-collector for the ferry district, that section of town facing Salem across the estuary. This was Thorndike's modest political debut. He was re-elected the following year to the same post.

In an earlier chapter we have followed the man's early steps in politics from constable to delegate to the Constitutional Convention of 1788, and from the Federalist success of that convention to the lower chamber of the General Court later in the same year. Thorndike did not participate very actively in political affairs while his own Federalist Party was in the saddle and in an apparently impregnable position. But after the Federalists received their signal defeat in 1800 and Thorndike saw his interests and his cherished beliefs alike mortally threatened, he emerged from his complete absorption in business and fought to keep the party alive in Massachusetts.

Jefferson was able to lead the Republicans to victory in the national election of 1800 as the result of a number of factors. The difference of opinion between Adams and Hamilton over

the handling of the threatened war with France in 1799 divided
the Federalists into two bitterly antagonistic factions. This split
within the party might still not have proved ruinous had not
the Federalists taken advantage of their position as the party
in power to pass some incredibly shortsighted legislation aimed
at consolidating or even perpetuating their majority by making
it unlawful to criticize or attack them in the press. Jefferson
capitalized on the blunder of the Sedition Law, and on the
additional folly of the Alien Law of the same time, and the
party was turned out. It is probable that Federalism was doomed
anyway because its adherents were suspicious of the mass of
the electorate and favored a restricted rather than an expanded
participation in government by the lower economic groups, but
the party's behavior hastened the evil day.

The reaction of Massachusetts Federalists was not to waste
time in vain lamentation, but rather to pitch in and reorganize
the party. The caucus system set up after the defeat put control
of the party in Massachusetts in the hands of the potent and
secret permanent Central Committee, which directed the activities of a hierarchy of county and local committees with marked
effectiveness.

Israel Thorndike was fully committed to this Federalist
renaissance, and he entered the open arena of contest for office
and served behind the scenes almost certainly as a member of
the Central Committee. Massachusetts politics was carried on
at a low personal level, and our first introduction to Thorndike's
political activities after the 1800 debacle reflects this. In the
Israel Thorndike Papers is a letter dated April 13, 1801, from
James Burnham, Parish Clerk, expressing appreciation for the
gift of one hundred dollars to the church (the Second Parish of
Beverly) and politely hoping that the donor would not take
serious offense at the comment in "Carlton's Register." The
arch-Republican *Salem Impartial Register*, which was the news-
paper referred to, had a field day over the contribution.

It is reported that a celebrated mercantile character
in a neighboring town, whose *integrity* has never been
questioned, has generously presented one hundred

Dollars to a certain parish, celebrated for *concord* and
unanimity of sentiment, ostensibly to promote their
music, and for *white washing* their house of worship—
but more probably to influence voters of the same parish
at the approaching election. Strange if these honest
People can be influenced by this trash—the *wicked Toll
of poor Mechanic's Bills* which said righteous man takes
care always to deduct!

Thorndike was elected to the Massachusetts House of Representatives at the Beverly Town Meeting of May 10, 1802, to
begin a legislative career that was interrupted only once in the
next thirteen years, and then only when he changed his residence
from Beverly to Boston, in 1810. The Federalists had squeaked
into office in Massachusetts even in the Jefferson Year, 1800, but
in 1802 they began a remarkable comeback under the leadership
of Governor Caleb Strong. Thorndike came into office on this
ground swell of favorable public opinion and remained there
even after Federalist popularity receded.

Thorndike was not a brilliant member of the legislature.
He had never cared for speech making and, judging by his
record of indifferent attendance in the House, he cared little
more for listening to the speeches of others. As was noted by
contemporaries at the Constitutional Convention of 1788, his
gifts lay more in committee work and informal persuasion. The
legislature made use of Thorndike's knowledge and experience
in commercial affairs. He was handed a number of minor
committee assignments dealing with money matters. In 1802–03
he was one of the appointed group that reported favorably
on Governor Strong's request that the Federal Government
reimburse the commonwealth for $41,679.78, the value of stores
taken over when Castle Island in Boston Harbor was ceded to
the United States in June 1798. He was also on several incorporation committees, a considerable chore in the days before uniform
corporation laws, when every company had to be considered
separately by a legislative committee. One corporation which
he himself petitioned to establish while in office was the Beverly
Bank.

Thorndike was on the committee that acted on the petition of William Gray, Jr., of Salem to incorporate the Essex Fire and Marine Insurance Company. Other concerns whose petitions for charters he dealt with included the Middlesex Canal Company, the Boston Bank and the Newburyport Bank. Perhaps it was as part of his initiation as a new state representative that he was assigned to look into the 1803 reappearance in the hopper of that hardy perennial, Samuel Blodget's appeal to sell lottery tickets.

Israel Thorndike closely followed the fortunes of his party in national politics. His reactions to the fate of the Federalist program are indicated in his correspondence. Writing to his English business associate, Thomas Dickason, Jr., on March 5, 1802, he observed that

> . . . party spirit rather increases in this Country & the present ruleing party are loosing the confidence of the federalist daily nor does Gallatin's *report* or his and the parties official conduct inspire additional confidence in our public funds. You have or undoubtedly will have rec'd intelligence of the Repeal of the judiciary, & the Meditated blow on the internal tax. I refer you to the speeches in Our national legislature for particulars which I think discover a genius that an older Country would be proud of.

It is to Thorndike's credit that he so far put aside partisan spirit as to point with satisfaction to the successful working of American political democracy. He sent his British friend copies of the addresses on both sides of the debate, although, as a staunch Federalist, he must have deplored the repeal of that revenue (and patronage-loaded) measure, the excise tax, as well as the repeal of the "midnight judiciary" law by which the lame duck Federalists had made a final desperate effort to retain some power through creating twenty-three new judicial districts and filling the resulting offices with their own people.

Thorndike's showing at the Beverly Town Meeting of 1803 was markedly less flattering than that of the previous year, but he was re-elected to the state legislature as runner-up to Joseph Wood. At that same meeting he was among the petitioners for a new road in Beverly, a Town Way. At a meeting that fall he was made both a grand and a petit juror for the Supreme Judicial Court.

In the 1803–04 sessions of the General Court, Thorndike was not very active, but he found time to serve on the committee that incorporated Nathaniel Fellowes and others as the Union Insurance Company. He also voted against the proposed Twelfth Amendment to the Federal Constitution, and thus went on record as favoring the old system of making the recipient of the second largest number of votes in a presidential election the Vice President, even though it was more than likely that he would be of the opposite party to the chief executive.

It must not be forgotten that the primary loyalties of these early citizens of the republic were to their local institutions and constituencies. In March 1804, Thorndike accepted election as fire warden in Beverly, an office to which he was elected for six consecutive years, as long as he remained a regular resident of Beverly.

In 1804 and again in 1805, Thorndike was elected to the state legislature. His record was not impressive. Home in Beverly, he continued to take his fire wardenship every bit as gravely as he did the more important office and participated actively in the deliberations over the purchase of a fire engine for the town.

Israel Thorndike was a subsurface operator by temperament, and it is unfortunate that we cannot follow more closely the course of his political movements during these troubled years. The fiasco of the Burr conspiracy and the battle over the Louisiana Purchase were both issues in 1804, and Federalist strength in Massachusetts was on the wane.

Thorndike was returned to the House by his Beverly constituency in 1806, but the Jeffersonian party won out in the

state and Thorndike sat with the Opposition. One of his few
recorded votes that year was in favor of counting twelve votes
from Isleboro marked "Caleb Stoon" for governor as votes for
Caleb Strong. The motion lost, but the Federalist champion did
just manage to get back into office and face a hostile legislature.
Thorndike was appointed to the insignificant Committee on
Names, which listened to the petitions of individuals who wished
to change their names from William Chamberlain Hunt or
Samuel Williams or Thomas Legate, Jr., to something else.

In 1807, Thorndike went up from the lower house to the
Massachusetts Senate. Essex County elected Enoch Titcomb,
John Heard, John Phillips, Jr., Nathaniel Thurston, Israel
Thorndike and William Gray. Thorndike was the low man in
the voting in his home constituency. The state as a whole was
less favorably inclined toward the Federalist ticket, and this
time the party lost not only both houses, but also the governorship, with the election of James Sullivan, the former attorney-
general. The legislative sessions of 1807–08 must have given Israel
Thorndike a sense of profound frustration. His vote was
consistently with the losers. Almost the only time when he
appears to have gone along with the majority was in the not
overly momentous decision to postpone the contemplated in-
vestigation of the affairs of Harvard College until the second
session! Again and again the Federalists were snowed under by
the Republican majority. They were unable to stop the setting
aside of a series of courts-martial or to delete from the Senate's
Answer to the Governor's Speech a passage accusing the Federalists of seeking to bring the nation "under the dominion of a
foreign power" [Great Britain]. The Federalists had also to sit
by and watch the General Court of Massachusetts endorse
Jefferson's proposed amendment to the Constitution which
would allow the President to remove Federal judges from office
on the vote of a majority of the House and two thirds of the
Senate. The only recognition accorded Thorndike's experience
during this bitter legislative year was his appointment to succeed
his fellow Federalist Harrison Gray Otis on the Senate Committee on Fortifications.

THE EMBARGO

The Federalist Party was in a parlous state in 1807. This plight was general throughout the country, but it was particularly disheartening to the membership in Massachusetts because heretofore they had been able to count on the party's vitality in that commonwealth. Then came an eleventh-hour reprieve to postpone the death of Federalism for another decade. This *deus ex machina* was the Embargo on American shipping in the foreign trade, a measure pushed through by Jefferson on December 22, 1807. This Act was a sincere but misguided attempt by the President to keep the young nation out of further involvement in the Napoleonic struggle that had enveloped Europe and seemed to be on the point of spreading to the New World.

Bonaparte had embarked upon his Continental System, seeking to destroy Great Britain by shutting her off economically from the rest of the world. The British retaliated with their Orders in Council declaring a blockade of Napoleon's possessions and dependencies.

Each participant in this mortal combat between nations hoped to enlist American aid against its enemy, but Jefferson's answer was to call a plague on both their houses and induce Congress to forbid commerce with either of them or with any other power.

The prompt reaction of the Massachusetts legislature was to treat the whole affair of the Embargo as a partisan matter. The Republicans, with remarkable shortsightedness for the interests of the state's essentially maritime economy, gave a vote of confidence to the Federal Government. Thorndike voted "nay" with the minority.

Timothy Pickering, United States Senator from Massachusetts, an old-line Federalist with strong pro-British tendencies, a leader in the ultraconservative Essex County "Junto", sought to present the case against the Embargo to the Massachusetts legislature in a letter to Governor Sullivan. Sullivan, a Jeffersonian, did not communicate this message, whereupon the Federalists raised the hue and cry about the suppression and Otis moved in the state senate that the governor be required to give to that body any information concerning public affairs received by him from one of the United States Senators from Massachusetts. The motion naturally lost, with Israel Thorndike once more support- ing the losing side.

But soon the fortunes of the Federalists once more began to brighten in Massachusetts. The distress and decline in business brought on by Jefferson's Embargo were pinching. The Re- publicans were voted out of office and the Federalists regained control of both houses of the legislature, though the Republican incumbent, James Sullivan, was returned to the governorship.

Israel Thorndike dropped back into the lower house in this election in the spring of 1808, but he continued to represent his Beverly district.

One of the first actions of the jubilant Federalists was to read out of the party the United States Senator and future President John Quincy Adams. This was a logical enough move in view of Adams's pro-Jefferson record, but one hardly calcu- lated to promote party harmony. Israel Thorndike's relations with Adams were mixed. When Adams attacked the Federalist leaders in 1828 and accused them of knowledge of, if not actual complicity in, Burr's conspiracy of 1804, and further accused them of plotting to divide the republic at the time of the Embargo, Thorndike naturally thought that he was one of the persons under attack. Along with such leading Federalists as Otis, T. H. Perkins, William Prescott and Daniel Sargent, and the sons of party leaders since dead, Thorndike signed a vigorous denial of the old man's charges.

On the other hand, Thorndike is known to have entertained John Quincy Adams at his house after this unfortunate exchange and to have sought a general reconciliation among the aging partisans. This attempt was firmly rebuffed by the die-hards, including Pickering, but it suggests that Thorndike's political differences with Adams did not carry over into personal relation- ships.

With the return of his party to power, Israel Thorndike found himself once more on the winning side of a series of contests in the House. He voted with the majority at least three times to pass resolutions against the Embargo. Majority or not, however, the Federalists were unable on at least one of these motions to muster a two-thirds vote over Governor Sullivan's veto, and the administration in Washington remained uncensured. By the fall of 1808 it was clearly apparent that the authorities in the national government intended to stick to their guns and ignore the protests and petitions for relief that rose with increasing clamor from the stricken communities. In response to this situation, the Federalists of Essex County summoned the meeting which has been called the Great Topsfield Caucus of 1808. Delegates from the several districts of the county met on October 6 in the parlor of the Topsfield Stage House on the Salem and Chelsea Bridge Turnpike "to consider the alarming and ruinous conditions of public affairs." Talk ran pretty high and drastic proposals were submitted. Robert S. Rantoul, in "The Essex Junto—the Long Embargo—and the Great Topsfield Caucus of 1808," says of the leading spirits, "Pickering and Parsons, Thorndike and Lowell were the more aggressive; Dane and Cabot more cautious and uncertain."

The leaders at this gathering were, in general, men associated with the so-called Essex Junto, a group which has been accused of disloyalty to the republic stopping just short of open treason. The membership of the Junto is not a matter of unanimous agreement and it is difficult to assess precisely Israel Thorndike's connection with the group. It is clear, however, that while probably not one of the tightly knit inner circle, he was at least a fellow traveler of the Junto. C. R. Brown, in *The Northern Confederacy According to the Plans of the "Essex Junto,"* puts Thorndike in company with Daniel Sargent and William Sullivan as "men of known radical tendencies and thoroughly converted to Juntoism."

There are fragments remaining of what seems to have been an intensive correspondence between Israel Thorndike and Timothy Pickering, the Junto's voice and representative in the government at Washington. In this exchange Thorndike appears in the role of economic advisor to the group. The fidelity with which Thorndike's recommendations and observations on national economic affairs were repeated by Pickering in his debates in the Senate is worthy of notice. Thorndike's connection with Timothy Pickering went back several years and was destined to continue for the rest of his life. Thorndike was one of the group of prosperous Boston and Essex County business and professional men who put up the money in 1801 to buy Pickering's Pennsylvania acres and make it possible for him to return from his self-imposed political exile following his dismissal from John Adams' cabinet. Among the thirty-four subscribers were Thomas Handasyd Perkins, Theodore Lyman, David Sears, William Prescott, John Lowell, Jr., and James Lloyd, Jr. The largest single subscriber was William Gray, Jr., of Salem, who put up two thousand dollars for twenty shares. Thorndike's contribution was five hundred dollars. Nothing could have been more poetically appropriate than that these lands should have been deeded in 1804 to a committee set up to use them on behalf of the children and family of Alexander Hamilton, who were in straitened circumstances following the calculated killing of the Federalist leader.

On November 23, 1808, shortly after the election of James Madison to the Presidency, Thorndike outlined for Pickering in some detail his estimate of the course of America's maritime trade if the Napoleonic Wars continued but the Embargo were lifted. Pickering rose in the Senate on November 30 to speak against the Embargo and quoted Thorndike's communication verbatim, with its promise of prosperity if only the disputed measure were repealed.

The Federalist majority in the Massachusetts House of Representatives took great satisfaction in getting some of its own back. They reversed the vote on Jefferson's proposed constitutional amendment concerning the removal of Federal judges. They endorsed an *Answer to the Governor's Speech* which contained some highly prejudicial references to restrictions on commerce. They voted to accept the report of the committee charged with receiving the petitions of the maritime towns regarding their distress under the Embargo. In all of these votes Thorndike went along with the majority. He also supported the report on the Republican governor's attempts to enforce the Federal Embargo with the state military establishment, a document which found those orders "irregular, illegal and inconsistent with the principles of the Constitution."

The elections of 1809 brought Israel Thorndike back to the Senate and the Federalist Christopher Gore to the governorship. The General Court was Federalist, and Thorndike's voting record reveals a consistently pro-British viewpoint, which he shared with a majority of his colleagues. This group was able to reject a motion to blame Britain for the "alarming state of foreign relations" and again to defeat a proposal to applaud Madison's action in demanding the recall of the insulting British envoy Francis James Jackson.

At long last the Embargo was repealed, and by the greatest irony, the Republicans were able to make political capital out of the abolition of their own unpopular piece of legislation and elect Elbridge Gerry to the governorship in 1810, as well as to make deep inroads into the Federalist majority. Thorndike was returned to office and, in an upsurge of popularity, commanded the greatest number of votes of any of the candidates in his Beverly district.

Israel Thorndike moved his legal residence from Beverly to Boston during this legislative year. This event was noted wryly by the Republican clergyman, William Bentley of Salem, in his diary entry for January 16, 1811: "The Great Mr. [Israel] Thorndike has left Beverly, in following the example of Mr. W[illiam] Gray, L. Gov. from Salem. As Mr. T. was unrivalled in Beverly & was sovereign it has been hinted that he did not appear satisfied to be lost among his many equals in Boston."

As a newcomer to Suffolk County, Thorndike did not enter the election for the General Court that spring. It was undoubtedly just as well for his blood pressure that he did not, because 1811 was the year of the great Republican landslide and both houses, under the leadership of the re-elected Gerry, engaged in an irresponsible orgy of partisan politics and spoils grabbing. Thorndike followed the events as a spectator, however, and may even have derived a grim satisfaction from watching the excesses committed by the incumbents, anticipating that these acts could only hasten a political overturn. Politics were freely discussed and debated at Thorndike's new Boston house at No. 6 Summer Street, and it is said that it was at Thorndike's dinner table that the celebrated "Gerrymander" political cartoon was first exhibited to ridicule bitterly the arbitrary manipulation of electoral districts by the Republicans in their wild urge to perpetuate themselves in office.

The hoped-for revolt of the electorate occurred and the 1812 elections saw the Federalists back in power in the Massachusetts legislature, with Caleb Strong once more at the helm. Israel Thorndike returned to the Senate that spring; it was his maiden term as a representative of his new Boston constituency.

PEACE OR WAR?

The primary national issue in the spring of 1812 was the imminence of war with Great Britain. The interests at stake were largely sectional and it is difficult to understand how purely partisan considerations led so many New Englanders to continue to support the Republicans, the war party. New England was bound to Old England by commercial ties of long standing. It is true that these had been strained by British Orders in Council during the Napoleonic Wars, but the losses from French seizures had been quite as intolerable as those from British attacks. Furthermore, New Englanders looked with alarm at the gobbling up of more and more of Europe by the rapacious Napoleonic armies. Most galling of all was the realization that the most vociferous urge to war came from the land-hungry Westerners, who hoped to annex Canada to the United States but who hypocritically chose to pursue their selfish ends under the guise of protecting the nation's maritime rights and interests!

A mass meeting was called in Boston to consider the threat of war. It was held at Faneuil Hall on the morning of June 11, 1812. Daniel Sargent offered two resolutions which were adopted: first, that it was necessary to avert war with England; second, that a committee of twelve be set up to consider and report measures to be adopted by the citizens of the town of Boston to that end. Israel Thorndike was appointed to the committee, and with him such figures as James Perkins, Samuel Dexter, Harrison Gray Otis, Charles Jackson and William H. Sumner. Before any action could be taken, President Madison had the satisfaction of seeing Congress declare war on Great Britain on June 18, 1812.

New England seethed. Parson Bentley said of the situation that August: "So high are parties that Lieut.-Gov. Gray having said he would willingly expend all his wealth in defence of the Government, Israel Thorndike, lately of Beverly now of Boston replied & he would as willingly spent all to oppose it." The Federalists knew that they were outnumbered in the country at large, so they attempted to combine with insurgent Republicans to support an antiwar Republican for the Presidency. It was agreed to call an informal forerunner to the modern national political convention in New York early in the fall of 1812, and in August a committee chose the Massachusetts delegation, which included Israel Thorndike. Nothing came of the convention, and the New England Federalists were reduced to purely regional activities to hamper the prosecution of the detested war and embarrass the national government.

In addition to resisting Federal appeals to call out the state militia, the New England antiwar partisans took advantage of their strategic financial position to sit on their accumulated piles of specie and let the Treasury peddle its depreciated securities as best it could. This policy was later partly abandoned, however, and Israel Thorndike, in a letter to Harrison Gray Otis, provided an adroit rationalization for subscribing to the Federal issue of April 1814.

Confidential
Philadelphia 23d. Apl. 1814
My Dear Sir
I have not done myself this pleasure since I left Boston because I have not had it in my power to com-

municate anything more than you would receive through
the newspapers, & other sources, & for other reasons that
will be obvs to you.

I arrived in this City on Monday morning, last,
since which I have been with Mr. Hare & some others
of your friends many times & have had much conversation about the loan, & have been made acquainted with
the doings, & opinions in Boston on that subject but
I will suggest to you a few thoughts for your consideration. I believe that a peace will actually take place before
next fall, indeed I think it almost certain, & if I am
right in this opinion can it be for the interest of any set
of men in this country who have anything at stake to
destroy public credit, which would, in my opinion, lessen
the value of all property & extend its effects to private
credit, under those impressions, & believing as I do that
the Govt. will have offers for 3 to 5 mln. & that they have
other resources, such as feeding the market from time to
time with their stocks, sending an agent to Europe
which *is* contemplated to sell stocks, against which they
will anticipate by passing their bills of Exchange, &c. &c.
they will, in my opinion, keep along untill peace takes
place, still however they would rather make a bargain
here for all they want & if any person or persons should
think it for their interest to treat with the Govt. for it,
the most favourable time would be directly after they
shall see that proposals have been made for a *small part
only,* now under those circumstances the question presents itself whether Federalists can, without any derelic-
tion of *principle,* can take any part in this loan, & if
they can whether it will be for their interest to do it, for
my own part I should think they might on the belief
however that peace is certain & that the public &
private interest would be promoted by it and the only
difficulty that I have on my own mind on the subject
is to reconcile the *apparent* inconsistency of the thing
& to satisfy the Federal party generally that it was right

in principle which I am aware would be difficult to do & without it could be done I would not as one, have anything to do with it, & my object in writing to you on this subject at this time is to beg the favr. of again calling your attention to the subject, & if you think proper, consulting some of your confidential friends, but without using my name, after which you will please to write Mr. Hare & inform him that you have recd a letter from me, & what will be the result of your own opinion & that of your friends upon this subject, this information from you to Mr. Hare is necessary because the gentn. here will wish to be informed sooner than they can have any information from me after my return to Boston which time is uncertain because somthing will depend on my stay in N York & more on the state of the roads which are horrid beyond description, I shall have this on monday morning in my own carriage with Post horses, Colo. Pickg accomps. me.

I am aware that the foregoing opinions respecting the loan &c. may lay me liable to the charge of inconsistency as *has* been the case in *Boston* respecting the opinions I gave at Washington as to the *effects* of the repeal of the nonimportation system, in which I still think I was perfectly correct, & I feel very confident that the sole object of the Govt. was the Revenues that would be derived & they do not care a fig who imports the goods while they git the revenue, now if you will sanction a systim the object of which is to raise revenue, which revenue *may* be appropriated to the expenses of the war, & without which it could not be continued, I do not see why the same persons should not advocate or furnish the loan, but for my own part I would do neither, if the war is to be protracted by it, but as I do not believe that it would I would do the latter if I could make a good bargain by it, & at the same time not counteract the wishes or opinions of my friends. Perhaps I ought to give some explanation respecting the opinion I hold as to the removal of the Embargo & nonimportation systim. I thought that the question ought to have been divided & that part of the Embargo systim which was complained of as unconstitutional ought to have been repealed, but upon the Idea that the President thought it for the interest of the countrey to reccommend it, & the govt. to lay it, it had not been in opperation so long as to cure them or their friends of their madness, and as to the repeal of the nonimportation at this time, it threw the whole trade exclusively into the hands of Neutrals or British subjects under Neutral colours who can have facilities, by licenses &c. from the British govt. which an American citizen cannot have without subject himself to heavy penalties & his property to seizure, thus I say all you git is revenue & that revenue will assist the govt. to carry on the war if they choose so to do. Please to tell Mrs. Otis & your family that their numerous friends in this place have charged me to communicate much of their respect & friendship to them, in which I most cordially join, & am in Great haste

> Your sincear friend
> and obt Servant
> ISRAEL THORNDIKE

HON H G OTIS

FEDERAL SECURITIES

Israel Thorndike's solicitude for the public credit was motivated by mixed considerations. As a conservative businessman, he favored a sound national monetary policy, and as an investor in government securities over a considerable period of years, he had a very real interest in protecting the value of his capital.

The entire picture of Thorndike's operations in the United States Treasury loan market cannot be reconstructed from this distance in time, but it is clear that at various periods he was an active trader. The Treasury records show that as early as 1792, Brown & Thorndike held U.S. 3% stock to the value of $4,388.61. Two years later they acquired funded 6% stock amounting to $2,041.64. At the turn of the century Thorndike was making considerable purchases for his own account. He began quietly buying $1,500 in funded 6's in the summer of 1799. The following year he bought more heavily, this time on the Royal Exchange of London, through his correspondents, Thos. Dickason & Company, who caused eleven U.S. stock certificates, totaling slightly less than $20,000, to be transferred to him.

In June 1801, Dickason & Company bought U.S. 6's for Thorndike's account—two certificates, No. 11,758 for $13,457.47, and No. 1577 for $6,000. The former he sent to Tristram Dalton to have transferred to his record on the government books, and the latter he sent to Bailey & Bogert of New York for the same purpose. On May 31, 1802, Thorndike instructed his London agents to purchase $25,000 worth of U.S. 6's for his account, exchange on England being below par and dull. He thought that they should be able to get the stock for 95% of par. This deal was apparently consummated, because in September he sent Tristram Dalton three certificates valued collectively at $26,829.66 to be transferred to his record on the Treasury ledgers. Two of these certificates, totaling $16,829.66, were deferred stock, while the third, for $10,000 even, was 6% stock. This time we are fortunate in having official confirmation of the transactions in the Treasury books themselves, now preserved in the National Archives. The New York office of the Treasury noted on October 6, 1802, entries to Thorndike's account of the indicated amounts. That same month he authorized the purchase in London of U.S. stock to the value of $15,000 when it fell to 98 or lower. The following February he dispatched three certificates, $11,650 worth, to be registered to his credit on the Treasury books.

On March 28, 1803, Israel Thorndike decided to unload his portfolio of U.S. stock and get out of the market. Accordingly, he wrote to his New York brokers, Bailey & Bogert, ordering them to sell his holdings. These he listed at a nominal value of $46,926.42, of which $30,096.76 was in 6's and the balance of $16,829.66 in deferred. He estimated that after the "extinguished part" had been deducted, these stocks should fetch about $40,000.

Two months later, on May 21, 1803, Thorndike wrote to Thos. Dickason & Company in London that he had disposed of his government securities but wanted to replace them in part now that prices were down. He put in an order for $20,000 to be invested in U.S. 6's if they could be got for 90% of par, certainly for not more than 91%, and then only if there were no immediate prospect of a resumption of hostilities between Great Britain and France. We have no record of any purchase, and since the pause in the Napoleonic conflict was brief, it is probable that the money was not invested.

The next record of Thorndike's trading in United States securities is found in the books of the New York office of the Treasury under date of January 14, 1812, when a purchase of $5,893.38 was entered. The records are not complete and it may be that this was the total of his holdings on April 23, 1814, when he wrote to Otis that he had had a change of heart and was no longer disposed to boycott the Federal security issues. It then remains an open question what weight should be attached to what motives in trying to explain this about-face.

There is no indication that Thorndike promptly went out into the market and subscribed to the loan of 1814. The following year, after the war was over, he did buy government securities. The Treasury books show that he acquired $25,000 worth of funded 7's of 1815 in July of that year, and $10,000 worth of funded 6's of 1815 that same August. He finally bought some 6's of 1814, but not until April 1816, a year and a half after the close of the war; so none of his Federalist friends could accuse him of inconsistency!

THE WAR OF 1812

Israel Thorndike was re-elected to the Massachusetts Senate with the great Federalist victory of 1813.

Although Boston Federalism had cheered to the echo the defeat of Napoleon in the Russian campaign of 1812, and Thorndike had been one of numerous "vice presidents" at a banquet at the Exchange Coffee House to celebrate that event, the Federalists showed no inclination to be similarly routed in a foreign war. They opposed the War of 1812, they favored Great Britain in her struggle with France, but they were of no mind to be caught unarmed and have the towns of the Massachusetts coast taken like sitting ducks. Early in the first session of the legislature Thorndike voted with the majority to memorialize the Federal authorities to provide the armaments of war for the citizens of the commonwealth. The Secretary of War ignored the problem posed by the defenseless position of Massachusetts, so the General Court undertook to organize its own defense. Israel Thorndike was appointed to a joint committee of the two legislative bodies to consider the "present state of discipline and practical knowledge in the art of gunnery of the Artillery Companies in this Commonwealth."

Throughout the legislative years 1813–14 and 1814–15 the Federalist majority in the state senate was continually torn between these two positions, their antiwar and anti-Napoleonic sentiments on the one hand, and their resolution to defend their homeland on the other. Thorndike's voting record reflects this dualism time and time again. One day the Senate set up a committee to see to the illumination of the State House "in commemoration of the signal deliverance of the Christian World from military despotism" with Bonaparte's collapse at the end of March 1814. Two days later they appointed Thorndike to another joint committee "to inquire what further measures, if any, it may be expedient to adopt for the defense of the Commonwealth."

In the fall of 1814 patriotic considerations had somewhat of an edge on party principles and Thorndike was busy with preparations for the defense of Boston. The nature of these defenses and Thorndike's part in their disposition is outlined in a letter, almost a report, sent to Timothy Pickering in Washington.

Boston 8th October 1814

DEAR SIR

Your favs of ye 28th. 29 & 30th ulto. has been duly rec'd & Contents Noted. The two last I have laid before the Comr the contens of which have been very acceptable to us all and your recommendations respecting the rations has been particularly attended to.

The works on Nodles Island are nearly finished & so are those on Dorchester hights but those on Dorchester point & on the neck are barely begun, I have with Genl. Brooks & Colo. Perkins been been on the dift grounds proposed to be fortified several times, the profiles were put up on the neck some time since & the plan you recommend has been adopted. I have also visited Governors Island where much has been done & more doing, & I think that forts Warren & Independence will be so strong that they will be able to repel any force that can come against them.

The secretary of the Navy has ordered a part of Bainbridges men to Portsmouth which has made him very angrey, & has induced him to offer to return the 6 32 pound cannon which he borrow'd from us some time since, saying that he has not men sufficient to fight his Guns they will be no use to him, he still keeps his Ships in the back ground, where they are to be protected by the Town, I should be Gratified if you will have some conversation with the secretary of the Navy on this subject & let him know the feelings of the people in this section of the Countrey upon this subject, the whole is familiar to you I therefore do not dwell upon it.

The Legislature has been together but 3 or 4 days, you will have been in possesn. of the Govs. Message before this reaches you I therefore do not enclose it, but I do the/the report of the Committee upon it.

The Govr. & Council have call'd on the Commissioners several times for their opinion as to the number of troops necessary to be kept up by this state.

Would things remain as they now are I am inclined
to believe that the Legislature will Order to be inlisted
about 2000 men to Serve during the war, & also to inlist
from 5 to 10,000 men that shall be properly officered
& organized, & shall be obliged to turn out once a month
at least for drill & military discipline, & always hold
themselves in readiness to march at a moments warning,
for which they shall be intitled to some small pay say
¼ to ⅓ full pay, & when call'd into actual service to
receive full pay, something like this has been thot on
with many other projects, I will thank you for your
opinion

As the Govt. of the U States refuse to pay the
expence of any troops which are call'd out to defend
the state unless it be such as are requested to be
detach'd by the officers of the U States, & Organized
agreeable to the arrangement made by the War depart-
ment, & which is dift. from the U S Militia law, & as this
whole systim is very unpopular with the Militia of this
state, I do not see but we must organize some state
force for present defense saying nothing of *ulterior
objects*. Should any thing of interest take place, I will
write you again to morrow. In the Mean time I am with
much respect

Your Obedient humble
servant
ISRAEL THORNDIKE

HON MR. PICKERING

(Italics added.)

THE HARTFORD CONVENTION

While it is mildly paradoxical to discover Israel Thorndike,
the case-hardened Federalist, engaged in the anti-British business
of fortifying Boston, the really arresting phrase in his letter to
Senator Pickering of October 8, 1814, is the reference to "ulterior
objects" for having an independent Massachusetts Army. What

motive could there be for establishing a state force not subject to Federal control beyond the "present defense"?

It would be rash indeed to build too heavily on this one cryptic passage from an exasperatingly ill-preserved correspondence, but secession was in the air, and Pickering was its arch exponent. Secession involved the threat of resistance from the rest of the union in 1814, just as it would in 1860. Nor was it illogical for a "solid" bourgeois like Thorndike, a man of property and eminent respectability in the community, to be moved by the radical views of a Pickering. Thorndike was an amateur in politics. Fundamentally, his life was tied up in his business. Until circumstances and a shift in the regional economy compelled a change, his preoccupation was with maritime commerce, and had been ever since he was a boy. He had started with nothing and achieved considerable eminence as well as a fortune by skillful attention to seaborne trade. Now for a decade and a half the national administration, largely representing the selfish interests of other sections of the country, had seemed intent upon the destruction of all the things that had made him important. What future lay ahead for New England and New Englanders, dependent upon commerce, in a political union in which the odds were so hopelessly unfavorable?

Four days after the letter on the defense of Boston was written, Thorndike voted with a majority in the Massachusetts Senate to send a delegation of twelve to a convention of the New England states to be held at Hartford, Connecticut, to confer upon common grievances and methods for alleviating these ills.

The story of the Hartford Convention has often been told. At its deliberations the extremists were thwarted by the moderates and secession was averted. John Lowell, a stalwart of the Essex Junto, had misgivings about the prospects of the radical cause beforehand. He wrote to Pickering a fortnight before the sessions opened—the letter is quoted in the *Life and Letters of George Cabot*—and gave the opinion which he had formed after looking over the list of delegates.

It is to be regretted that we had not chosen two or three such persons as Daniel Sargent, William Sullivan, and Colonel Thorndike. I do not know that we have among the delegates a single bold and ardent man. I know it will be said that such men are not the fittest for counsel. That is perhaps true in common times; but in times of great trouble they are often the most proper, and, indeed, the only ones fit to direct and manage affairs.

With the coming of peace, the chief popular support for the convention was removed and the Republicans jumped at the chance to discredit its whole conception and smear the men who had participated in its deliberations.

The decisions of the Hartford Convention did not just wither away, however. The delegates proposed seven amendments to the Federal Constitution, embodying a program reflecting the whole purpose of the convention but excluding the wild-eyed aims of the Essex conspirators. These amendments sought to protect the New England states from a recurrence of the evils which they felt had plagued them since the opening of the century. These measures were presented to the Massachusetts legislature at the second session, early in 1815, during Israel Thorndike's last term in the General Court. It is not surprising to find in Thorndike's voting record a complete endorsement of the Hartford Convention and its legislative program.

On January 26, 1815, Thorndike voted to approve a resolution in support of the proceedings of the convention. Within the next fortnight he voted "yea" with a majority of the Senate to (I) abolish slave representation in the national legislature, (II) require a two-thirds vote in both houses of Congress for the admission of a new state to the Union, (III) limit embargoes on foreign commerce to sixty days' duration, (V) require a two-thirds vote of both houses of Congress for a declaration of war, (VI) prohibit naturalized citizens from holding Federal office and, lastly (VII), limit the Presidency to a single term and prohibit one state from providing two Presidents in succession. On proposed constitutional amendment IV, which called for a two-thirds vote of both houses for passing nonintercourse laws, there was no division of the Massachusetts Senate.

Of the seven articles, only one has been added to the Constitution, and that only in part. As the result of political feelings quite as strong as those which prompted the calling of the Hartford Convention, the Presidency has been limited to two terms.

These were the last important measures to be voted on by Israel Thorndike, and may be regarded as his legislative swan song.

The anticlimax of the Hartford Convention did not remove its participants from public life. Timothy Pickering continued to represent his constituents, and Thorndike continued to advise him on economic affairs.

THE TARIFF OF 1816

In the summer of 1815, Thorndike was astonished to receive a communication from the Republican Secretary of the Treasury, Alexander J. Dallas, sounding him out on the tariff question. The party in power had not been noticeably concerned with New England Federalist opinion on economic—or any other—matters, but Thorndike was prepared to meet a conciliatory gesture in kind. He wrote Pickering about it on the last day of the year.

> Mr Dallas sent to me, as he did to many others, a circular letter requesting my opinion on the subject of a new tariff of duties, & after much reflection I made up my mind to answer his letter, & to answer it in the same manr. & the same temper as though we had a Federal administration & that the public debt had been contracted by a wise & virtuous governmt. because we cannot git along without establishing the public credit

however injudiciously it may have been managed, & I cannot give you a better knowledge of my view of the subject than by sending you a copy of my letter to Mr. Dallas, which I now enclose for your perusal.

Dallas was engaged at the time in preparing his celebrated report of February 12, 1816, recommending a protective tariff for the United States in response to the laments of the domestic manufacturers who had come into existence during the war and now found themselves hopelessly undersold in the peacetime flood of British imports.

Thorndike's proposals to Dallas, together with his subsequent recommendations to Pickering, reflect the opinion of the Boston maritime community on the tariff question. They also give some insight into the thinking on this subject of a new group with which Thorndike was becoming more closely associated, the New England cotton-textile manufacturers.

Thorndike wrote to Dallas on October 23, 1815, noting that his own health had been poor for some time—a fact which may explain his withdrawal from politics—and outlining a series of recommendations for the new tariff bill. He favored taxation primarily for revenue and noted that ease and sureness of collection were prime considerations. He outlined a detailed schedule of duties on produce of the Baltic area, Europe, West Indies, and China. The only protective section concerned woolen cloth. He said, "Wool manufactured ought to be charged with high duties because it will encourage the Agriculturist & manufacturer." To this he added a footnote: "Wool is a raw material which would be difficult to import in time of war. The farmer would be induced to increase his flocks & *improve* his breed, if he knew he was to be protected by high import duties on imported wool, while the manufacturer would be sure of a supply in war as well as peace."

Certain provisions suggested advantages to certain groups, such as the prohibition of imports from China in foreign bottoms, a bounty on exports of salt-cured provisions to equal the duty on the salt used in the curing, a bounty on exported spirits to encourage importation of molasses for rum and the raising of grain for whiskey.

The Dallas tariff bill was warmly debated in Congress in the spring of 1816, and by the middle of March the measure was brought before the House of Representatives. Thorndike wrote immediately to Pickering to protest certain sections of the bill and to suggest modifications favorable to the maritime interest. He opposed duties on cotton textiles as ruinous to the China trade, and particularly to individuals (like himself) who were actively engaged in that trade and who would sustain great losses if their vessels returned to the United States laden with cottons only to be confronted with a tariff so high that the goods could not be sold except at a loss. Pickering responded at once to Thorndike's plea for relief for merchants with East India voyages already in progress. On March twenty-sixth he rose in the House and, as reported in the *Annals of Congress*, ". . . made a few remarks in favor of relieving the merchants now engaged in trade, and in danger of ruin by the bill." Pickering put forward a stronger case on April third and was supported in the debate by Congressman Ward, also from Massachusetts. The result of this battle put up in the House by the Massachusetts delegation was that the tariff, as finally passed, contained a section embodying Thorndike's recommendation, and in language not greatly different from that suggested in his letter to Pickering of March twentieth.

Thorndike underlined his views on the proposed cotton-textile duties in a letter to Pickering of April first, and revealed therein an interesting reconciliation of the apparent conflict of interests between his role as an importer of Oriental cottons and his newer role as a New England cotton-mill owner.

Boston 1t. Apl. 1816

Dear Sir
Your ever esteem'd fav. of the 25th & 26th Ulto reach'd me by the last mail & for which I thank you. How far the new tariff meets with *Genl.* approbation

among the merchants I cannot pretend to say because (having been confin'd to my house for the most of the past winter & still go out but little) I have not been in the way of hearing much discussion upon the subject, I presume however that they feel as I do upon the main question, Viz that the Govt. have very foolishly contracted a heavy debt, & if we mean to exist as a Nation it must be paid, to do which taxes in *some form* necessarily follow, & the object ought to be to have them lev[ie]d in such way as to opperate as equally as possible & in such way as after they are once fix'd they shall be permanent, at least, untill the object is attain'd for which they were first laid. With this view of the subject, I am fully persuaded that the duty on imported coarse Cottons is too high, it will be a compleat prohibition, & will undoubtedly raise the price of coarse Cottons so high as to induce many persons to invest large capitals in this business, notwithstanding the uncertainty of the continuance of the same duty, the effect of which, I think, may be foretold & that is that the price demanded by the manufacturer will be so high as to occasion complaints from the consumers so the Govt. *may* be induced to listen to the popular voice, & take off the whole or so large a portion of the duty on Cottons as will blast the future prospects of the manufacturers, & have them to perish.

I am a considerable propriator in a cotton factory (with Mr. F Lowell & others) & *I* am decidedly of the opinion that it would not be for the *permanent* interest of that or any other of the kind to prohibit the importation of this fabric, for reasons before ment[ione]d but it does appear to me that those persons who are employed in forign voyages, & have already given orders which cannot be revok'd have a *right* to claim protection from the Govt. to save them from impending ruin, and I still think that a law so unjust will never pass without this saving clause at least.

To what extent were the views of Israel Thorndike and his friends embodied in the law as actually passed? In general, Thorndike's proposals did not fare too badly. He lost out on the protective tariff on cotton fabrics. Duties were required to be paid on cheap cottons at twenty-five percent for three years and thereafter at twenty percent. A preference was also shown for *ad valorem* duties, while Thorndike believed that specific duties were preferable because easier to collect. On Baltic products the final schedule tended to approximate that outlined in the letter to Dallas. West India items were taxed at low rates, as Thorndike advocated. Importers of European manufactured goods in general paid twenty percent; of dyestuffs, only seven and a half. In the China trade the principle of a differential in favor of imports in American-owned ships was maintained, as Thorndike desired, though not going so far as to exclude vessels of foreign registry from the American market. The drawback on exports of salt-cured foodstuffs was retained. Woolens were protected by the same scale of duties as cotton, and Thorndike had advocated protection to woolens. Mention has already been made of the provision to protect East Indies traders whose vessels were already at sea and committed to cotton cargoes at the time the new tariff law was passed.

The Act of April 27, 1816, did not go into the matter of Thorndike's other favorite project, the licensing of stills and bounties on exported spirits, but these matters were covered by subsidiary legislation very much as he had suggested, even to the granting of a preferential treatment to distillers of rum as compared with distillers of whiskey.

THE NAVIGATION ACTS

The Tariff of 1816 soon became a dead letter under the pressure of events. As McMaster says in the fourth volume of his monumental *History of the People of the United States*:

> Unhappily for the friends of domestic manufactures,
> the framers of the tariff had utterly ignored the im-

portance of an agent destined not only to break it down,
but to destroy the manufactures it was intended to protect, prostrate the importing and retailing business,
send tens of thousands of men into idleness and want,
and involve the people heavily in debt.

This powerful agent was the pent-up productive capacity
and carrying potential of England, now released by the defeat
of Napoleon. British manufacturers dumped heavily on the
American market and devised ingenious frauds for getting
around the tariff. Then, to complete the competitive advantage
of its nationals, the British government reapplied the old restrictions of the colonial system to trade with the British West
Indies and closed the islands to American ships. The provincial
governments of New Brunswick and Nova Scotia added to the
woes of the New England commercial community by imposing
export duties designed to restrict the trade in plaster of Paris
to Canadian bottoms. The cumulative result was, McMaster
adds, "to prostrate the shipping interests and bring back to
memory the days of the long embargo."

Naturally, the American shipping interests turned to the
Federal Government for help. On December 9, 1816, Timothy
Pickering wrote from Washington to Israel Thorndike in Boston
for advice on a proposal to vote an American Navigation Act
which would impose upon foreign vessels the same restrictions
and prohibitions which the foreign nations imposed upon American merchantmen. Thorndike's reply was most temperate. He
tended to favor the retaliatory proposals, at least on an experi-
mental basis, and expressed the belief that pressure of this kind
on Britain would lead her to open up an indirect, face-saving
connection with the United States because of the dependence
of her West Indian islands upon American forest products.

Pickering did not participate in the debates on the Navigation Acts, but Thorndike's arguments in favor of the legislation were put forward by two other congressmen from Massachusetts, Cyrus King and George Bradbury. Both brought out
his point of the probable yielding of Britain in the Caribbean.

The Navigation Act was signed March 1, 1817. It provided that after September 30, 1817, goods could be imported into the United States only in American vessels or in vessels that truly belonged to nationals of the country in which the articles originated. A related measure was also passed applying only to the plaster of Paris trade with the Canadian Maritime Provinces. These laws marked the beginning of the end of foreign navigation systems.

With the limited evidence available, it is impossible to assess Thorndike's influence upon the actions of Congress. What does appear clearly is the weight that his statements of the case for the maritime commercial group carried with the Massachusetts representatives of that group in Congress. It is also apparent that the reasonableness of his suggestions appealed to the larger body. There is a high degree of correlation between his recommendations and the provisions of the measures as they were actually passed, and from this it is clear that as regards commercial legislation, at least, Thorndike was in step with his times.

GOOD FEELINGS

Israel Thorndike was not a bitter-ender. The extraordinary aura of good will which enveloped Federalist New England upon the coming of Republican President James Monroe in the summer of 1817 affected Thorndike along with the rest. To cite McMaster again, "With the arrival of Monroe . . . the community suddenly realized that peace had removed old causes of animosity, and that issues which two years before had been vital were then extinct."

Thorndike's younger contemporary, Robert Rantoul, already quoted, recalling the events many years later, noted this mellowing: "Israel Thorndike, also a Federalist, was as violent a partizan, previous to the accession of Munroe, as any to be found in this part of the country, yet he was among the most forward in his attentions to Mr. Munroe in Boston and in this town."

The President was lavishly entertained in Boston and then

continued his triumphal progress up the coast to Portsmouth. He stopped off at Beverly as an honored guest of Thorndike. The *Salem Gazette* noted in its columns on Friday, July 11, 1817, that Monroe "Thursday morning breakfasted at an early hour with the Hon. Mr. Thorndike at his seat in Beverly, with a large company invited for the occasion." Even the sour William Bentley was impressed by the scale of the entertainment and actually got into the spirit of the Era of Good Feelings from the Republican side. He wrote in his diary on August fourth that Thorndike "came down and gave a superb entertainment to President Munroe . . ." and added:

> Col. Thorndike has been uncommonly successful & has rank in wealth & good sense with our first men. The whole display at Beverly was at his expense. He provided the ornaments at the bridge, the salute of the revenue cutter, and of the cannon on shore. Entertained in the best style 300 persons in his house, besides a much greater number abroad, & supported every ceremony.

THE MASSACHUSETTS CONSTITUTIONAL CONVENTION OF 1820

On Monday, October 16, 1820, a meeting was held in Boston to choose delegates to a convention called for the purpose of considering changes in the Constitution of Government of the Commonwealth of Massachusetts. Israel Thorndike was one of the forty-five representatives elected at the meeting.

The state constitutional convention of 1820 came about from the agitation that arose after the separation of Maine from Massachusetts and its admission to independent statehood. Public opinion demanded a change. Some individuals thought that there were too many members in the lower house of the General Court. Others found fault with the apportionment of state senators. There was dissatisfaction in some quarters about the third article of the state bill of rights, having to do with compulsory church attendance. The result of this restlessness was that the legislature submitted the issue to the people, and they voted to have the constitutional convention assembled.

It was a considerable gathering of notables from all parts of Massachusetts that gathered in Boston for the opening sessions on November 15. Most prominent of the group was former President of the United States John Adams, who was received with honors. It was hoped that he might preside, but the infirmities of his years prevented this. Robert Rantoul recalled afterwards, "I dined with him at a party at Col. Thorndike's. It was apparent that his mind was somewhat impaired by age." From this note we learn that Thorndike continued to entertain the important figures of the day at his house on Summer Street.

A fairly complete account of the meetings is provided by the *Journal of Debates and Proceedings in the Convention of Delegates Chosen to Revise the Constitution of Massachusetts,* in the form of a third-person paraphrase of each speaker's remarks, the whole set up in painfully fine type. The *Journal* is of peculiar interest to anyone concerned with the political career of Israel Thorndike, because it provides the only approximation to a verbatim account of any of his public addresses thus far discovered.

Thorndike expressed himself with the greatest fervor on the issue of qualifications for the franchise. Speaking with reference to a suggestion that all property requirements for voting be abolished,

MR. THORNDIKE, of Boston was in favor of but few alterations in the constitution and opposed to this. He rose to speak only of the practical effect of this provision in the constitution, so far as it had come under his observation. He had long been acquainted with the seafaring men in a neighboring town of about 4000 inhabitants, and had witnessed there the effect of the provisions in the constitution upon young men under age, which had been described by the gentleman from Concord [Hoar], yesterday [Monday, December 11], as operating upon young men engaged in agricultural pursuits. They were generally anxious to amass the little property

necessary to give them the right of voting, and this
anxiety had a favorable effect on their habits and character. The case of seamen had been alluded to as entitled to consideration. They had been described as men
who scatter a great deal of money and do not save
enough to make them voters under the constitution.
The votes of Seamen of that description he said, ought
not to be received. They were the votes of their owners,
or of intriguing men who wish either to get into office
themselves or to get their friends in. If the qualification
was not high enough to answer all the objects for
which it was intended that was no reason for rejecting
it altogether. It might be of great use. If frauds were
committed, measures might be taken to prevent them
and to obviate the objections on that ground.

The matter of the franchise was presented to the people
under the title Article Six, and the property qualification was
adjusted to exclude persons under guardianship and paupers
from voting.

One of the rejected amendments, Article Five, called for a
series of changes in the machinery for electing state senators
and representatives, and provided that members of the seven-
man state council should be elected by the voters at large instead
of by the legislature. Thorndike disagreed with the majority of
his colleagues on this last point and said so.

The question to be decided was what was the best mode
of selecting seven counsellors, so as to obtain men best
qualified. He thought the mode which had been ad-
hered to in practice under the constitution was the best.
Gentlemen had contended that it was liable to abuses.
He had for many years had a seat in the legislature,
and he had seen no such abuses. It was the most simple,
and he thought the most satisfactory mode. It was a
mode in which men best qualified from every part of the
Commonwealth could be obtained, and men most likely

to meet the approbation of the people. The people could
judge and compare their opinions in no other way so
well as through their representatives in the two branches
of the legislature. It was a power little likely to be abused.
It was the first act performed by them after coming
together from among their constituents. If they did not
consult the wishes of their constituents in the election
of counsellors, as well as in their other duties, they
could not again be elected to their seats. This could
give them a sufficient interest in consulting the wishes
of the people.

In the records of both of these discussions Thorndike is
found to hold consistently to the view that the fewer the
members of the citizen body allowed to participate in matters
of government, the better the quality of that government.

There was prolonged debate upon the church-and-state issue.
When an anticlerical delegate proposed to abolish the tax
exemption on the estates of clergymen, provided any such estate
exceeded one thousand dollars, Thorndike turned conventional-
minded. "Mr. Thorndike thought the legislature had full power,
and that it would be beneath the dignity of the Convention to
introduce any thing into the Constitution which should aim
at this useful and respected class of men, either to take away
any part of their privileges, or to hold them up to public
odium." On the other hand, while he went on record as being
essentially pro-cloth, he did not think that there was a great
deal to choose from between denominations. When it was moved
to empower an absentee landowner to specify which religious
group should benefit from the church tax on his property,
"Mr. Thorndike opposed the amendment. It was for the advantage of every estate that religious worship and moral and
religious instruction should be maintained in the town where
it was situated. It might be presumed that in the aggregate one
religious society would be as much benefitted as another."

Given Thorndike's general outlook and position, it is not
surprising to find him opposing a resolution providing that

"no Bank should hereafter be incorporated, nor the charter of any existing Bank renewed unless the Stockholders shall be liable in their private capacity." His stated objection does not, however, strike at the principle so much as at the wording: "MR. THORNDIKE opposed the resolution: It did not determine who were intended, the original Stockholders, or the Stockholders at the time of any defalcation."

Most of these questions, which so roused the delegates assembled, died with the convention, but not without giving us a further view into the beliefs, views and prejudices of various groups in the electorate, and particularly of Israel Thorndike of the Boston delegation.

SIX

Investments Ashore

TRANSPORTATION, INSURANCE AND BANKING

Israel Thorndike's first recorded participation as an incorporator was in the company formed in 1787 to build the Essex Bridge
between Beverly and Salem. This was one of a series of original
subscriptions to concerns related to transportation and communication. These utilities comprised the most numerous group
of corporate enterprises at whose birth he assisted, though they
were not the companies in which he invested the greatest capital.

After the Essex Bridge came the Salem Turnpike and Chelsea
Bridge Corporation, chartered in 1802 to connect Boston with
the settlements along the North Shore. A year later it was the
Ipswich Turnpike, from Beverly to Newburyport. Associated
with Thorndike here were John Heard, Stephen Choate, William
Gray, Jr., Jacob Ashton, Asa Andrews, Joseph Swasey, Nathan
Dane, William Bartlett and Joseph Prince.

In 1818, Thorndike was an original proprietor of the Massachusetts Bay Canal, forerunner of the present Cape Cod Canal,
and planned to connect Buzzards Bay with Barnstable Bay to
cut off the hazardous and time-consuming run around the cape
on the coastwise passage. The old guard of the Boston maritime
community was represented, but each venture attracted new men.

Thomas Handasyd Perkins, William Tudor, Jr., Uriah Cotting, John T. Apthorp, Henry A. S. Dearborn, Charles Davis and Thomas M. Jones went along with Thorndike on the canal.

Thorndike's first railroad venture was as a charter stockholder of the Massachusetts Rail-road Corporation, organized in 1830 with the stated ambitious design of connecting Boston with the Hudson River at Albany or Troy. This project reveals the early realization of the need to tap the hinterland, lest Boston be left high and dry by the success of her rival New York, already enjoying the benefits of the Erie Canal. As usual, some of the names of the investors are familiar ones among Thorndike's group of business acquaintances; others we meet for the first time in this context. Old friends are Harrison Gray Otis and William Prescott. New names are those of Joseph Coolidge, Francis J. Oliver and Phineas Upham.

More nearly related to the founding of the Cabot Manufacturing Company the following year than to the canal-building fever was Thorndike's participation in the Springfield Canal Company, chartered in 1831 to make use of the waters of the Chickopee River. There is a marked overlapping in the lists of incorporators of the two enterprises.

The only other railroad in which Thorndike had an interest was the Boston and Taunton Rail-road Company, organized in 1831 to run from Boston to Taunton, Massachusetts, and from there toward Providence, Rhode Island.

More closely related to his ownership of wharf properties, to be considered under the heading of real estate transactions, than to his railroad activities was his investment in the Boston Marine Railway Company. This corporation was chartered by the General Court on February 15, 1826, upon the petition of Caleb Loring, Nathaniel Goddard and Charles Tracy. The "railway" was a device for raising ships out of the water so that workmen might scrape their hulls, paint and effect repairs.

By far the heaviest investment Thorndike made in corporate shares outside of the textile industry was in insurance companies. This was consistent with his interest in underwriting, noted earlier. Paradoxically, however, less is known about his connection with the forming or managing of these companies than about the part he played with lesser enterprises. Perhaps he was content with the role of passive subscriber.

The final key to his portfolio is in the inventory of his estate. One fact appears somewhat surprising as one looks over the list of nontextile stocks Thorndike owned at the time of his death. He owned almost no shares in any of the companies which he had helped to found!

At the very time that maritime concerns were occupying so much of his attention and energies, Israel Thorndike entered upon an entirely new field of business. He became a banker. The Beverly Bank was chartered on July 23, 1802, with an authorized capital of $160,000. Thorndike was the first president and held that office until his departure for the larger world of Boston in 1810.

The bank occupied premises at the corner of Cabot and Central Streets in a brick building put up by John Cabot a few years earlier.

The affairs of the Beverly Bank were handled with the utmost conservatism and caution. A letter to a prospective borrower, dated May 18, 1803, states that the directors loaned money for sixty days or less provided the loan was secured by bonds or mortgages of twice the value of the amount borrowed. Undoubtedly the same rigid terms applied to the officers of the bank. On March 25, 1805, Israel Thorndike issued his personal promissory note to the President and Directors of the Beverly Bank, sixty days, for seven thousand dollars. The note is receipted May 27, the date the loan was repaid. Thorndike's own bank book shows that his account stood at $21,942.01 at the end of 1807.

Thorndike's connection with the Beverly Bank was not his only banking tie, although it was certainly his most intimate and practical banking experience. He also served as one of the first directors of the Boston branch of the First United States Bank.

At Thorndike's death he owned the following non-manufacturing stocks:

INSURANCE AND OTHER STOCKS

No. of Shares	Company	Value per Share	Total
100	National Insurance Co.	$ 49.75	$ 4,975
30	Commercial Insurance Co.	90	2,700
10	Hope Insurance Co.	95	950
79	Beverly Bank	62.50	4,937.50
91	Canal Bridge	75	6,825
10	Boston Marine Railway Co.	370	3,700
16	New Hampshire Iron Foundry	[62.50]	1,000
15	Springfield Bridge	90	1,350
10	Londonderry Turnpike	10	100
1	Massachusetts Bay Canal		—
10	Beverly Social Library	1	10
108	Androscoggin Bridge	35	3,780
1	Church in Purchase Street	10	10
100	Mass. Hospital Life Ins. Co.	112	11,200
1	Ten Hill Farm	[150]	150
20	Cattle Fair Hotel	50	1,000
10	Essex Turnpike	7	70
25	Salem Marine Insurance Co.	200	5,000
60	General Interest Ins. Co.	2	120

$47,877.50

THE COTTON MANUFACTURE

When Israel Thorndike mentioned to Timothy Pickering in his letter of April 1, 1816, that he was "a considerable propriator" in a cotton factory "with Mr. F. Lowell and others," he was referring to his participation in the operations of the Boston Manufacturing Company, established in 1813. It will be recalled that this was not Thorndike's first venture into the textile business; he had been one of the founders of the short-lived Beverly Cotton Manufactury back in the late 1780's. The Beverly venture had been an experiment. The new concern, born of the protected domestic market of the War of 1812, was an altogether different type of enterprise from its very inception.

The advantages enjoyed by the Boston Manufacturing Company derived primarily from the fact that its backers had almost unlimited financial resources and were not hampered by the artisan's concern with day-to-day mechanical problems. They were the more adventurous members of the merchant class, who were not content to sit tight while their mercantile businesses were ruined by embargoes and war. They faced the unpleasant realities and saw the need to turn their capital to some entirely new productive activity. They entered the textile field not to make cloth, but to make money. They were prepared to hire the technical know-how and pay well for it. They had not acquired their capital by hand-to-mouth methods. They had resources, energy, executive ability and general business experience in large-scale, highly competitive fields.

The original act of incorporation of the company, signed February 23, 1813, authorized the issue of four hundred thousand dollars' worth of capital stock. Seven years later an increase of capitalization to eight hundred thousand dollars was approved. The minute-books of the concern in the Baker Library of the Harvard Business School show that the proprietors agreed to begin by selling one hundred shares at one thousand dollars each, the payments on these shares to be made in installments as needed and called for. On September 4, 1813, the proprietors, listed in the order of the size of their holdings, were as follows:

Stockholders	Shares
Patrick Tracy Jackson	20
Francis C. Lowell	15
Israel Thorndike	10
Israel Thorndike, Jr.	10
John Gore	10
Charles Jackson	10
James Lloyd	5
James Jackson	5
Nathan Appleton	5
Uriah Cotting	5
Benjamin Gorham	3
Warren Dutton	2
	100

On April 3, 1815, it was decided to sell the second hundred shares, with the stipulation that each proprietor could purchase as many new shares as he had original shares and, in three years, could acquire twice as many additional shares as he was now buying of the second issue. Most of the original proprietors stayed on the escalator, doubling their holdings on the list of October 3, 1815, and redoubling them as of May 9, 1817. The Thorndikes, father and son, held on with their friends and came up with holdings of 40 shares each.

The fourth issue, that of February 1820, brought in a number of new investors, with the Thorndikes and Nathan Appleton as the only heavy purchasers of the old group. Shares of the fourth issue sold at $1,150, a premium of $150 a share. Thorndike now emerged as the third man in the company in number of shares owned. P. T. Jackson and F. C. Lowell each held 80 shares to Israel Thorndike's 60. Lowell soon died and Thorndike stepped up into second place. He subsequently gave up 22 of his units to Lucy Cabot, Dr. James Jackson and others, and held 38 at the time of his death in 1832. Meanwhile, with the death of John Gore, Thorndike was elected president of the corporation at a meeting of the stockholders on May 7, 1817. He held this position with the company for the next fourteen years, until just a few months before his death.

The Boston Company, often referred to as the Waltham Company because of the location of its plant, developed early into a fully integrated manufacturing establishment. Spinning, weaving, bleaching, dying and other processes were carried on in a single mill, and to these was added the production of textile machinery as a side line. This organization marked a striking advance toward modern industrial practice.

The company solved the labor problem by setting up a group of company-operated boardinghouses in which the daughters of farmers were assured of respectable surroundings when they came in from the country to work in the mill for a few years prior to marriage. The concern was thus rendered independent of the local labor supply, and the coming of the dismal "mill town" blight, so prevalent in British textile centers, was postponed in New England for a generation.

The Boston Manufacturing Company prospered almost from the outset. At the first annual meeting presided over by Israel Thorndike and convened at his store at 45 India Wharf, Boston, on October 7, 1817, it was voted to declare a dividend of $170 a share, a return of 17 percent on the investment. Thereafter the earnings record remained quite impressive, though becoming less regular toward the end of Thorndike's administration.

Year	Dividend
1817	$170
1818	125
1819	125
1820	150
1821	200
1822	275
1823	250
1824	250
1825	300*
1826	80
1827	90†
1828	120
1829	75
1830	70
1831	110

* Includes $150 in profits from sales of machinery.
† Includes October dividend of $50 a share voted by the proprietors in the absence of a quorum of directors.

An employee profit-sharing scheme was put into effect early in the company's existence, and certain managerial employees were voted blocks of stock. As early as 1819 it was decided to simplify the company's marketing procedure by selling its entire output to a single distributor, B. C. Ward & Company. Nine years later the concern entered into a sales agreement with J. W. Paige and Nathan Appleton for the joint marketing of the products of the Boston Manufacturing Company and those of the Appleton, Hamilton and Merrimack Companies, which had been established in the meantime.

Early in 1822 the company made arrangements with Kirk Boott to construct the machinery for the Merrimack Company, then being organized to do business in Lowell, Massachusetts. In 1823 the machinery-manufacturing branch of the Boston Company was turned over to the Merrimack Company and the shops were moved to Chelmsford, Massachusetts.

The owners of the Boston Manufacturing Company increased their investments in the cotton-textile industry and expanded their operations during the 1820's by the establishment of new concerns. The interests of the Boston and Merrimack Companies were united following negotiations carried on late in 1821, and the proprietors of the older company voted to accept Boott's offer and acquire one hundred and fifty shares of the stock of the new company, distributed on the basis of one share of the new for four shares of the old. Purchases by individual shareholders were optional, and Israel Thorndike did not go along with his colleagues in the new arrangement. The inventory of Thorndike's estate shows, however, that he subsequently acquired a substantial block of Merrimack stock and held 100 shares, valued at $1,000 a share, in the appraisal of July 3, 1832.

At the meeting of the directors of the Boston Company on December 19, 1822, Samuel Crocker and Charles Richmond of Taunton, Massachusetts, were authorized to build textile machinery by using the company's patents. Just a month later the Taunton Manufacturing Company was incorporated by the legislature, with Israel Thorndike, Sr., and Israel Thorndike, Jr., as the only proprietors of the Boston concern listed among the incorporators of the new company.

In 1825, Thorndike joined with his associates of the Boston and Merrimack Companies and some new investors to establish the Hamilton Company. His initial investment was the purchase of 50 shares. Three years later some members of the old syndicate took in more new investors to form the Appleton and Lowell Companies. Thorndike bought 40 shares of the first and 30 shares of the second.

Participation in textile activities in the newly built town of Lowell, Massachusetts, was virtually inseparable from partici-

pation in the company that controlled the source of power for
the mills in that place, the Proprietors of Locks and Canals on
Merrimack River. A list of major shareholders in the Locks and
Canals, dated February 28, 1825, and preserved in the records
of the corporation at Lowell, shows Thorndike in third place.

Stockholders	Shares
Nathan Appleton	92
J. W. Boott	80
Israel Thorndike	76
C. Gore	66
P. T. Jackson	60
Israel Thorndike, Jr.	60
James Jackson	40
J. A. Lowell	40
Charles Jackson	40

Israel Thorndike's interest in organizing new textile-manu-
facturing companies continued right down to the end of his life.
In 1829 he joined with Samuel Cabot and Robert G. Shaw to
petition the General Court for a charter for the Grafton Manufacturing Company, organized to produce cotton, woolen and
linen cloth at Grafton in Worcester County, Massachusetts. In
1832, the last year of his life, he became an incorporator of the
Cabot Manufacturing Company at Springfield. Associated with
him in this venture were several Boston men of substance who
had hesitated to commit their funds to textile manufacturing
before it had proved itself sound. They were prepared to take
the plunge at last and capitalization was authorized up to a
million dollars. Besides Thorndike, the founders of the Cabot
Company were Jonathan Dwight, Harrison Gray Otis, Edmund
Dwight, James K. Mills, Thomas Handasyd Perkins, S. A. Eliot,
Benjamin Day, Samuel Cabot, Francis Stanton, George W. Lyman
and George Bliss.

For a final accounting of Israel Thorndike's investment in
the textile business, we refer once more to the inventory of his
estate filed on July 3, 1832. It was to the manufacture of cotton

cloth, primarily, that Israel Thorndike shifted the greater part of his interest, energies and accumulated capital during the last decade and a half of his life, and his business career thus embodies the economic shift of New England—away from the sea, and from commerce to manufacture—which characterized this period.

The inventory lists textile-company shares as follows:

MANUFACTURING STOCKS

No. of Shares	Company	Value per Share	Total
38	Boston Manufacturing	$ 700	$ 26,600
100	Merrimack	1,000	100,000
30	Chicopee	1,000	30,000
56	Cocheco	600	33,600
50	Hamilton	1,100	55,500
40	Lowell	900	36,000
40	Appleton	1,050	42,000
30	Suffolk	1,150	34,500
50	Cabot	50	2,500
63	Taunton	200	12,600
76	Locks and Canals	1,050	79,800
			$453,100

The story as outlined, coupled with these figures, gives substance to the comment on Thorndike in Stone's *History of Beverly:* "He was also an early patron of manufactures, and invested, it was said, a greater amount of capital in them than any other individual in New England." It also supports part of the statement in *Hunt's Merchants' Magazine:* "When commerce began to be taxed with heavy duties, he at once invested a large portion of his large capital in manufacturing establishments, which he early saw would be the true policy of New England."

BOSTON REAL ESTATE

Israel Thorndike moved from Beverly to Boston in 1810, but he had owned real property in the metropolis for several years prior to making the move. Quite naturally, in his Boston real-estate ventures he was motivated by all of the usual considerations. He acquired property to use in his mercantile business, for his home and its surroundings, for investment on a rental-income basis, for investment to sell. There were times, too, when it was useful to have something tangible to put up as security for a loan when funds were needed for other enterprises.

Boston in Thorndike's day was an inverted pear-shaped peninsula of high ground thrust into the Charles River basin. It was edged with wharves on its eastern, seaward side, flanked with marsh and mud-flats to the west, and connected with the mainland by a narrow stem at the south. Thorndike's real-estate holdings fell into four main groups: waterfront property, property on Summer Street and Otis Place, the John Hancock estate on Beacon Hill, and miscellaneous commercial premises.

Thorndike first bought Boston real estate because he needed another base of operations besides his warehouses and office at Beverly. In 1804 he paid five thousand dollars for a brick store at No. 8 India Wharf. Three years later he purchased No. 20 for seven thousand dollars, and within the fortnight he paid Harrison Gray Otis eight thousand for the premises at No. 45 India Wharf, which was to be his Boston business address during the years 1818–1825. In 1815 he bought eight shares in the Central Wharf and Wet Dock Corporation, and in the division of the property, early in 1817, he bid in No. 53 Central Wharf, which was to become his business address for the later years of his life. Central Wharf was an imposing structure a hundred and fifty feet wide projecting almost a quarter of a mile out into the harbor. Down the middle of it ran a row of stores four stories high. Space which Thorndike did not need in his own business, he rented out to other merchants.

Thorndike's most important single real-estate undertaking in Boston was centered on the property just up the hill from the waterfront on Summer Street and Otis Place and adjacent areas in the shadow of the Wren-like spire of New South Church. He began acquiring this land from Thomas Russell's heirs late in 1809. During the next five years he built the section into a very substantial holding. The assessment records reveal that the initial assessment of twenty-six thousand dollars, which corresponded to the purchase price, was gradually built up to more than one hundred thousand dollars in 1817 and reached a peak of $187,800 in 1826.

The method of handling this enterprise was to buy the land and build brick houses on it and then rent them out. Vacant lots are listed in the earlier records, but between 1812 and 1819 these are replaced, first by unfinished houses, described as such, and ultimately by the names of the lessees of the completed buildings. This whole area was destroyed in the 1872 fire, but early photographs preserved by the Bostonian Society in the Old State House show the houses to have been severe examples of the late Georgian town house with chaste doorways and undecorated façades. Thorndike's tenants remained in these houses year after year, with very little turnover. Names that remain on the assessor's lists of householders over a long period are those of William Ropes, William Prescott, Israel Thorndike, Jr., George Bond, John Tappan, Bryant P. Tilden, John C. Gray. Nathaniel Bowditch lived in a Thorndike house for a while, and so did Kirk Boott. By far the most celebrated of the tenants was Daniel Webster, whose name first appears in the assessor's "taking books" in 1825.

The relationship between Daniel Webster and Israel Thorndike is obscure. There seems to have been great intimacy between the two men and their families, but it is undoubtedly because they lived near enough to talk face to face and had no need for written communication that the details of this friendship are lost. Webster lived at No. 10 Summer Street in 1825, and Thorndike lived next door at No. 11. We know that the Thorndikes and the Websters were closer than ordinary neighbors, because on June 16, 1825, when Lafayette came to Boston to lay the cornerstone of the Bunker Hill Monument, Webster held a great reception in his honor and a doorway was cut through the party wall between the two houses so that the guests could surge freely from one house into the other. Sometimes the guests came from the other side. In the *Life, Letters and Journals of George Ticknor* we find that Ticknor wrote to Webster on February 2, 1826, "We went the other night to a great ball at

Colonel Thorndike's, a part of which extended into your house." The sole reference to Israel Thorndike in that extensive accumulation, *The Private Correspondence of Daniel Webster,* is the note in a letter from William Sullivan dated March 23, 1830: "As to mere town news, Mr. Thorndike is said to be much indisposed." At least, Sullivan knew that this item of gossip would interest Webster, though at this date they were not such close neighbors, since Thorndike had moved to No. 40 Summer Street by 1829.

In 1826, Thorndike began to unload some of his Summer Street holdings, beginning with the sale to John Tappan of the house on the corner of Summer and Arch Streets for twenty-one thousand dollars. John C. Gray paid eighteen thousand dollars for No. 9 Summer Street. Houses along Arch Street sold for less; prices ran from five thousand eight hundred dollars, the usual figure, up to seven thousand dollars.

The inventory of Thorndike's estate shows that at the time of his death in 1832 he owned real estate in this section valued at more than one hundred and thirty thousand dollars.

In 1821, Thorndike began buying up lands on Beacon Hill, adjoining Mr. Bulfinch's new State House, as this property was sold off piecemeal by the heirs of John Hancock. The process continued until 1825, by which time he had acquired an undivided twenty-seven fifty-ninths interest in a tract with 232 feet 2 inches frontage on the north side of Beacon Street, facing the Common. Hancock's handsome Georgian house was still standing on the land at this time.

In 1825 Thorndike petitioned the court to subdivide the jointly held property. Just as soon as the partition was effected, he began selling off this property. The parcel immediately adjoining the State House and to the west of that building was sold to Augustus Peabody for forty thousand dollars, which must have come in very handily to pay off a mortgage in a like amount to the Merchants Insurance Company of Salem just a month later. The Hancock tract was entirely disposed of during Thorndike's lifetime.

The largest single business property listed in Thorndike's estate is the Commercial Coffee House on Milk Street, corner of Liberty Square, in the heart of the business district which was still focussed on the docks, valued at thirty thousand dollars. Before acquiring a clear title to this inn, Thorndike had leased it from David Sears. It sheds some light on the business methods of the time to learn that by an agreement entered into on September 22, 1825, the quarterly rental for the Commercial Coffee House was commuted from the earlier payment of eight tons and five hundred hundredweight "first quality of wheat or Indian corn" to eleven ounces, two pennyweight and one grain pure gold.

This picturesque survival suggests another practice to be noted occasionally among the records of Thorndike's real-estate transactions. On several occasions he was the sender or recipient of a formal "Notice as to light and air." Such a notice reminded the owner of adjacent premises that he was forbidden by law to enjoy the advantages of light and air secured by cutting a window through the wall of his house overlooking the other's property.

Other items in the category of quay-side commercial real property were various store buildings on Market (later Cornhill) Street and South Market Street with a combined value of twenty-six thousand dollars in 1832.

It is hard to say whether property valuations, real and personal, provide a valid index of an individual's possessions or merely reflect the general level of prosperity and the vagaries of the taxing authorities. Presumably, such figures, examined over a period of time, have some usefulness in charting a property owner's relative worth, provided they are used with caution. Statistics are available, if one is prepared to take the trouble of going through the assessor's records ward by ward and adjusting for the relocating of ward boundaries for Israel Thorndike's Boston holdings during the last twenty years of his life. In 1811, the first year after he came down from Beverly, his real property was assessed at $30,000; his personal property, including merchandise, ships, the contents of his houses, and the like, was listed at $150,000. By 1817 the figures were up to $100,000 and $230,000, respectively. In 1822 he had slightly under $185,000 in real and $275,000 in personal property. Five years later, in the peak year 1827, his real estate was assessed at $205,000 and his personal property at $400,000, although the real-property value had fallen off $75,000 from the previous year because of his extensive sales of houses and lots. From this dizzy height the totals fell off irregularly until stabilized at about $200,000 for real estate and $230,000 for personal property.

SEVEN

The Older Thorndike

PERSONAL RELATIONS

What sort of man was Israel Thorndike to do business with as he sat in his countinghouse directing a web of transactions that covered the globe?

In his role as employer he appears as two distinct individuals. On the one hand was the almost patriarchal head of a large family of mariners, with a fatherly concern for each. On the other was the cold, hard, self-made executive who had got to the top by keeping an eye cocked for the main chance and never relaxing his purposefulness for an instant.

The first, more sympathetic side is manifest in his kindly concern for the welfare of the widow of one of his captains, Eleazer Giles, who was left in straitened circumstances by her husband's death. This is expressed in a letter dated July 24, 1810, to a third person acting as agent.

I have seen and conversed with the widow of the late Capt. Giles who I am sorry to say is left in rather indigent circumstances and of course it is very important to her and her family the the most possible should be made of what Capt. Giles left. An impression seems to

be made on the minds of the heirs that Capt. Giles had
much more property than appears that he had from the
statement which you make, and they seem to fear that
all the property which he left never came into your
hands, and that some of it had been lost or plundered
before it came to your hands amongst which is ment-
[ioned] his beding and cloathing, which they say was
valuable, none of the former and very little of the latter
has ever come to hand, not even to the value of £5 stlg
in all. I tell Mrs. Giles that so far as you have any agency
in this unfortunate business she may depend on haveing
justice done her, and that I would write to you and
request of you to git all the information possible as to
the detail of the accounts, inventory of the property,
cloathing and so forth and what had become of them
and therefore will thank you to furnish to Mrs. Giles
every information, in detail, that you can. From inquiry
I fear that there is no insurance on the Brigt. that can
be recovered, but I should suppose that Mrs. Giles can
and will if necessary pay £200 stlg if you should be
unfortunate in the sute now pending in the appeal, I
have assured this *good* unfortunate Lady that you will
do all in your power to promote her interest, and I pray
that you will make every exertion to produce a favorable
issue in the cause now pending and that as *soon* as
possible that this family may be relieved from the sus-
pense under which they labr. . . .

This solicitude for the families of his employees is apparent
also in the handling of the recurring item, the appeal from a
seaman's wife for news of her man or money to tide her over
until his return. There are a number of such pathetic communications scattered through the Thorndike correspondence, usually
with an annotation in a later hand that the amount had been
sent. One Lydia Manning wrote in for ten dollars on September
4, 1797, against the amount due her "husban," Thos. Manning.
She asked for and received an additional five dollars the follow-

ing January twenty-ninth, when she spoke of an illness. Similarly, Elizabeth Swan addressed a communication to Colonel Thorndike on February 21, 1799, requesting news of her "husban" and funds. She was sent five dollars.

Thorndike's less attractive side must have been widely recognized in his own day. An article about the "colonel" that appeared in the *Beverly Citizen* half a century after his death and tended, if anything, to eulogize the late merchant-shipowner, expressed it like this: "He was quick in his decisions, firm in his conviction, not easily provoked; but when he considered himself imposed upon, he was terribly passionate; rage could hardly have expressed it."

A startling example of this wrath—a consuming, corrosive, irrational fury, which burned for years, even after the death of its object—is found in the case of Captain Samuel Hill of the ship *Packet*. For some reason Thorndike conceived the idea that Captain Hill was cheating him on voyages in the copper trade between Chile and Canton by carrying freight on the *Packet* for his own personal advantage. We have two sources for this story. One is the naturally one-sided account contained in a nineteen-page letter written by the unhappy Hill to John P. Cushing, the prominent Canton merchant; dated Boston, March 8, 1823, it is preserved in the *Thomas Handasyd Perkins Papers* at the Massachusetts Historical Society. The other is the record of the Court of Common Pleas in Boston, noting the dismissal of Thorndike's lawsuit against Hill that charged a violation of owners' orders.

Hill says that when Thorndike conceived these suspicions, he went on board the *Packet* upon her arrival in Boston Harbor and proceeded at once to interrogate the crew. He interpreted his findings as corroborative evidence. The carpenter, for example, was sure that Hill was making money on the side, because, he said, he had nailed up some gold specie and silver bullion in boxes. The mate, Crocker, and the assistant mate, Robinson, according to Hill's account, saw a splendid opportunity to advance themselves at Hill's expense, so they allowed themselves to be convinced by Thorndike that Hill was defrauding his owners. Sumner, the second mate, refused to play along with the others and stood by Hill. Hill told Cushing that Thorndike was so irrevocably committed to proving him in the wrong that he was prepared to go to great lengths to shore up his case, and to keep from losing face by having to retreat from his original accusing position.

Crocker confessed to Hill that he was convinced that Thorndike had actually altered entries in the *Packet's* cargo book to "prove" Hill's malfeasance. Hill's horror is expressed to Cushing:

> Could you my Dear Sir, have believed that a man who holds a place amongst the Honorable of our Country, a man who Ranks amongst the Dignified & Wealthy Merchants of these United States, could so far forget himself as to sacrifice every principle of Humanity as well as of Truth, to support a Cause which he knows to be a bad one merely to gratify his obstinacy or his Vanity . . .?

Hill goes on to say that his books of account were happily in perfect shape; it was merely a secondary record that was tampered with. When it became obvious that there were no grounds for prosecuting Hill for fraud, Thorndike sued him for fifty thousand dollars for disobeying orders. The lower court found for Hill and awarded him costs. But Thorndike did not rest. He appealed, and the appeal was continued from term to term of the Supreme Judicial Court until the second Tuesday of November 1826. By this time Samuel Hill was dead and the action was directed against his estate. On the indicated second Tuesday, Elizabeth Hill, widow of the captain and administratrix of his estate, failed to come into court in Boston from her home out in Framingham and so defaulted. The higher court then reversed the lower court's decision and awarded Israel Thorndike damages of five thousand dollars from Hill's estate. Elizabeth Hill seems to have quietly declined to accept the higher court's ruling, so Thorndike entered a new suit against her and on March 25, 1830, won a judgment of $5,911.66 and $55.27 for costs. The court records do not reveal whether or not Thorndike ever actually laid his hands on the money.

Resorting to the law was not a new experience for Thorndike. He was litigious by nature, a not uncommon trait during his period. He was fully accustomed to legal action before he ever left Beverly, and the Suffolk County Court of Common Pleas dockets contain Thorndike cases for every year that he lived in Boston, beginning in 1810, the year he moved to town. Most of the cases have to do with the collection of debts, usually on promissory notes. The records are incomplete, but about a third of the time he recovered from the defendants.

No amount was too large or too small to be the cause of suit if Thorndike felt strongly in a situation. In 1812 he sued Henry Higginson, principal, and Stephen Higginson *et al.,* trustees, for $110,000 for merchandise allegedly consigned to Higginson in London but not accounted for. This was settled out of court. At the other end of the scale, he sued one Mathias Hiler, laborer, for a debt of $60.90 and recovered.

There is other evidence than that of the Samuel Hill case for believing that Thorndike could be a hard man in money matters. In November 1826 he sold to his former employee, Captain Isaac Stone, the brig *Israel* for eighteen thousand dollars, that sum to be paid in installments over a three-year period, and the debt to be secured in the meantime by a bottomry bond for twice the value of the vessel, or thirty-six thousand dollars. In the course of the three-year period Stone and Thorndike became involved in an entirely separate transaction involving a consignment of pig iron valued at about five hundred dollars. In the course of this second deal Thorndike sued to recover the iron and received a judgment for the value of the iron. But since Stone was using all of his earnings to pay for the brig *Israel,* he was unable to pay the judgment, so Thorndike attached the ship and then turned around and sued to recover the thirty-six-thousand-dollar bottomry bond because Stone was failing to meet his payments. In 1831, Stone presented his case before the Supreme Judicial Court of the Commonwealth in a chancery hearing. Again, as in the Hill case, we have only the argument of the defendant, this time in a formal legal brief submitted to the chancery court. Stone asked that only nominal damages be granted to Thorndike, on the grounds that Thorndike's attachment of the vessel in the unrelated pig iron case prior to the expiration of the three-year-term of the bottomry bond constituted a total loss quite as much as though the brig had been lost at sea. The document made it clear what Stone's estimate of Thorndike's motives was: "The Def[endan]t being unable to make any arrangements what ever with said Thorndike to repossess himself of said ship, and the said Thorndike apparently intended that he should not have her again, he was compelled to come to said Thorndike's terms, and give up the ship to him, and execute a bill of sale to him. . . ." The case continued for some years after Thorndike's death and on February 6, 1838, was settled in favor of the executors, with a judgment for $8,208.75 and $113.34 costs.

Israel Thorndike was not himself immune to legal action, although he was defendant less frequently than plaintiff. William Gray sued him in 1816 for $150,000, the stated value of twenty-seven boxes of silk goods and brandy shipped from Bayonne, France, to Boston on the ship *Volant*. It was brought out in court that the *Volant* had been taken prize by the British, so the defendant was charged only with costs, $582.42.

In 1822 the Supreme Judicial Court decided against Thorndike in an action brought against him by the guardian of John H. Gray for failure to deliver seven shares of West Boston Bridge Corporation stock. The judgment came to about four thousand five hundred dollars. Later that same year he lost a case in which he was sued for a small sum by one Thomas E. Moore, a seaman on the brig *Hindu*.

The legal cases are not of great moment in themselves, but they help to round out the picture of Thorndike in his dealings with his contemporaries.

GIFTS AND BEQUESTS

When Israel Thorndike died in Boston on May 8, 1832, "expiring calmly, though suddenly, in the bosom of his family," as Stone's *History of Beverly* puts it, he was found to have left an estate appraised at $1,133,401.52.

During his lifetime he had been a fairly steady but not a lavish donor to various causes. His gift of one hundred dollars to the Second Parish of Beverly has already been remarked upon. He subsequently gave the First Parish some real property from which it was able to realize twenty-six hundred dollars, and the present of an "elegant chandelier for its vestry."

Thorndike had received almost no formal education, but he made several gifts to Harvard University. He was one of the larger subscribers of the one hundred forty-seven who contributed to the Massachusetts Professorship of Natural History, established March 25, 1802. His donation was five hundred dollars, paid in two installments. Josiah Quincy says that in 1818 he also gave five hundred dollars toward the library of the Theological School.

Unquestionably, Thorndike's most important single benefaction was the purchase in 1818 of the library of Americana of Professor C. D. Ebeling of Hamburg, Germany, from an agent of the King of Prussia. This library he proposed, in a letter addressed to the President and Fellows of Harvard College and read at their meeting of June 26, 1818, to give to Harvard. This letter, together with the reply of acceptance, is quoted here through the courtesy of the present President and Fellows.

DEAR SIR,

Having been informed, some time since, that the late Professor Ebeling of Hamburgh had left a very extensive & valuable Library containing many volumes, maps & charts, peculiarly adapted to be useful in the United States, I determined upon purchasing it, provided it could be obtained at a fair price, considering its intrinsic worth, & to present it to the University at Cambridge as a mark of the great esteem I feel for those who compose the government of that Seminary & of veneration for its great antiquity & usefulness. You will perceive by the enclosed letters & copies that this object has been effected, & that orders have been given for the shipment to the United States for acct. of the University.

I have to request that your Corporation will be pleased to accept this Library, with my best wish that it may be found conducive to the great end we all have in view, the extension of knowledge in our country.

I wish, however, to reserve for my own use any duplicate or triplicate copies of works &c which it will not be of any decided advantage to the College to possess. I am, Dear Sir, with respect

        & esteem your obedt. servant

This substantial (for 1818) gift brought forth a considerable flow of eulogy and rhetoric. Sidney Willard, who attributed this and the good works of several other nineteenth-century benefactors of Harvard University to the friendship and benign influence of the Reverend Joseph Willard of Beverly, waxed quite eloquent on the subject:

> Why did Israel Thorndike in the year 1818, purchase the Ebeling library at the cost of six thousand five hundred dollars, rescued from the grasp of the King of Prussia? . . . Because [he] had wisdom enough to perceive and patriotism enough to feel, that such vast additions of books pertaining to the history of this continent were all-important, and that the opportunities were to be seized now, forthwith; that, if they were suffered to pass, they were gone for ever. . . .

The Harvard authorities recorded their acceptance of the gift in a resolution remarkable for its flowery prose style. It was voted: "That the Corporation most gratefully accept this donation to the University. They beg leave to express to the Donor their high gratification in this act of munificence, which entitles him to the respect and gratitude of present & future times . . ."

The final word on the Ebeling gift, and on Thorndike as a donor, was written by Sidney Gunn in the entry on Thorndike in the *Dictionary of American Biography*: "As this was his largest public gift, although he left an estate of $1,500,000, and the outlay was only $6,500, he cannot be considered a pioneer in philanthropy."

Israel Thorndike wrote the greater part of his will in 1830. It consisted of thirty-one numbered sections. After directing his executors to pay all his just debts and legacies, he devoted several paragraphs to making provision for his third wife, Sarah Dana Thorndike, daughter of the Reverend Joseph Dana of Newbury-port. He had married her in 1818, a year after the death from dysentery in her fifty-third year of his second wife, Anna Dodge Thorndike. (Since Thorndike made several charitable contributions in 1818, it is possible that Sarah Dana might have had some influence on his essentially self-centered thinking.) The widow was to receive her clothes and jewelry, two brick houses on Summer Street, Boston, her choice of the interest from a fifty-thousand-dollar trust fund or an annuity of twenty-four hundred dollars (to be discontinued if she remarried), the horses and carriages, fifty dozen bottles of Madeira wine, and the use of Pew 86 in the First Parish in Beverly "forever."

A trust fund of twenty thousand dollars was set up, under the direction of the Massachusetts Hospital Insurance Company, to be untouched for fifty years and then distributed among the heirs.

A series of specific bequests took care of distant connections, cousins, and so on. Jonathan Town, Thorndike's huge coachman and confidential servant, was to receive six hundred dollars; this was subsequently raised to a thousand dollars in a codicil.

Generous provision was made for Anna Thorndike Loring, wife of William J. Loring, a daughter.

All of the children were to share in certain trust funds, but in the division Andrew fared less well than some of the others, and the sons of the deceased Edward, out in Ohio, were to get very little indeed.

The chief beneficiaries of Israel Thorndike's will were his sons Israel, Jr., Charles and Augustus.

There must have been some popular expression of disapproval when the terms of the will became known in Boston, because of the defensive tone found in Bridgman's *The Pilgrims of Boston and Their Descendants*. His figures are exaggerated and the account is inaccurate, but the editorializing is highly suggestive.

> To three sons he bequeathed each about half a million dollars, and other sums to another son, to his widow, and daughters; in all about eighteen hundred thousand dollars to his relations. Some poor man may be inclined to say that were he the owner of one or two millions of dollars, he would bequeath much to the great charities of the world; but perhaps on gaining the power he would lose the disposition to benefit others beyond his own family, and would forget that of them to whom much as the stewards of Heaven had been given, much will be required.

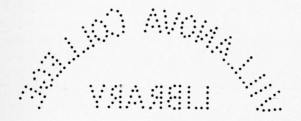

Bibliographical Note

The principal source of information for this study of the life and business career of Israel Thorndike is the *Israel Thorndike Papers,* an extensive collection of letters, bills, memoranda and other documents in the Baker Library of the Harvard University Graduate School of Business Administration.

Another primary source for all phases of Thorndike's activities, business, political and personal, has been the manuscript collections of the Massachusetts Historical Society. The collections of the Beverly Historical Society and the Western Reserve Historical Society in Cleveland are important in specific fields. The Dana, Dane, Henry Knox, H. G. Otis, T. H. Perkins and Timothy Pickering papers in the M.H.S. are particularly rich in Thorndike material. The *Beverly Shipping MSS.,* particularly the *Nicholas Thorndike Papers* at Beverly shed light on the early maritime story. The Kirtland letters in Cleveland are the chief source of material dealing with the venture in Western lands.

The minute-books of the directors and of the proprietors of the Boston Manufacturing Company in the Harvard Business School Library provide the story of that concern and Thorndike's part in its management.

Certain public records have also been of great value. For material referring to Thorndike's early life, the probate records and deeds of Essex County, Massachusetts. For evidence of his political activities, the Beverly Town Records and manuscript *Journals* of the two houses of the Massachusetts General Court. His real-estate transactions are found recorded in the deeds of Cuyahoga County, Ohio; Hancock County, Maine; and Suffolk County, Massachusetts. The National Archives have yielded information about his investments in United States securities, via the Secretary of the Treasury's records; and about his maritime commercial affairs, in the records of the Customs District of

Salem and Beverly. The records of the Court of Common Pleas in Suffolk County and the Supreme Judicial Court of Massachusetts, together with the probate records of Suffolk County, reveal much about Thorndike's contacts with the law, including references to the contents and disposition of his estate.

These manuscript records have been augmented, especially for the larger scene, by the more readily available published series of public records, the *Vital Records of Beverly, Annals of Congress, United States Statutes at Large* and *Acts and Laws of the Commonwealth of Massachusetts,* and by various documents relating to the French Spoliation Claims in the records of the United States Court of Claims and the Senate and House Miscellaneous Documents.

In special areas certain secondary works have been most valuable. Mention has been made in the text of Dr. Octavius Thorndike Howe's paper, "Beverly Privateers in the American Revolution." To this must be added Gardner Weld Allen, *Massachusetts Privateers of the Revolution* (Boston: Massachusetts Historical Society, 1927) and volume 15 of *Massachusetts Soldiers and Sailors of the Revolutionary War,* a compilation from the archives published by the Secretary of the Commonwealth (Boston: Wright and Potter, State Printers, 1907).

Samuel Eliot Morison, *The Life and Letters of Harrison Gray Otis* (2 vols.; Boston and New York: Houghton Mifflin Company, 1913) disentangles the complexities of New England Federalist politics.

The story of the rising textile industry is related in Caroline F. Ware, *The Early New England Cotton Manufacture* (Boston and New York: Houghton Mifflin Company, 1931) and Melvin Thomas Copeland, *The Cotton Manufacturing Industry in the United States* (Cambridge, Mass.: Harvard University Press, 1912; Harvard Economics Series No. 8).

The standard accounts of the local scene are Edwin M. Stone, *History of Beverly* (Boston, 1843), and D. Hamilton Hurd, *History of Essex County, Massachusetts,* (2 vols.; Philadelphia, 1888).